THE

NORTH END

A BRIEF HISTORY
OF BOSTON'S OLDEST NEIGHBORHOOD

ALEX R. GOLDFELD

THE
History
PRESS

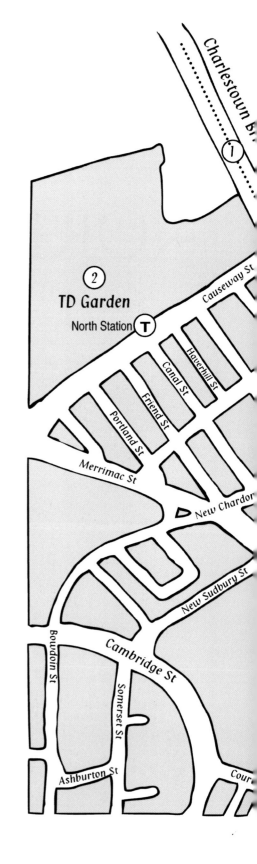

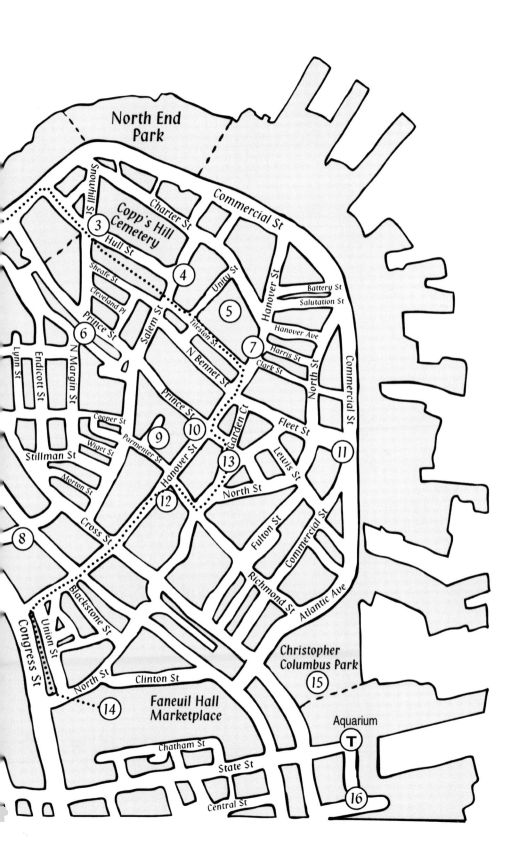

Published by The History Press
Charleston, SC 29403
www.historypress.net

Images are courtesy of the author unless otherwise noted.
Cover images:
(front, top) A View of Part of the Town of Boston in New England and Brittish Ships of War Landing Their Troops, 1768. Courtesy of the Boston Public Library, Print Department.
(front, bottom) One of the ancient buildings that awaited Irish immigrants, located at the corner of Lewis and North Streets. *Courtesy of the Boston Public Library, Print Department.*
(back, top) The John and Lydia Tileston House. *Private collection.*
(back, bottom) The Faneuil Hall market extension, 1827. *Courtesy of the Boston Public Library, Print Department.*

First published 2009
Second printing 2011
Third printing 2012
Fourth printing 2013

Manufactured in the United States

ISBN 978.1.59629.518.6

Library of Congress Cataloging-in-Publication Data

Goldfeld, Alex R.
The North End : a brief history of Boston's oldest neighborhood / Alex R.
Goldfeld.
p. cm.
Includes bibliographical references and index.
ISBN 978-1-59629-518-6
1. North End (Boston, Mass.) 2. Boston (Mass.)--History. 3.
Minorities--Massachusetts--Boston--History. I. Title.
F73.68.N65G65 2009
974.4'61--dc22
2009015380

Notice: The information in this book is true and complete to the best of our knowledge. It is offered without guarantee on the part of the author or The History Press. The author and The History Press disclaim all liability in connection with the use of this book.

To my wife, Mariel

CONTENTS

ACKNOWLEDGEMENTS

I gratefully thank my wife, Mariel Gonzales, for her unwavering support during the research and writing of this book. She indulged my obsessive interest in Boston's history and did not begrudge the time needed to write about it, despite her simultaneous pregnancy and the birth of our daughter, Risa.

For granting me permission to use their historical treasures, I sincerely thank Emily Piccolo, as well as the very helpful staff members of the following institutions: AP/Wide World Photos; *Boston Globe*; Boston Public Library; Bostonian Society; Georgetown University Archives; Historic New England; Massachusetts Art Commission; Massachusetts Historical Society; Museum of African American History; Museum of Fine Arts, Boston; New York Public Library; Norman B. Leventhal Map Center; Old North Foundation; Vilna Shul; and Woodstock Theological Center Library.

Special acknowledgment is due to those librarians and other keepers of the past who went out of their way to assist and encourage my work. They are Elaine Grublin and Laura Lowell of the Massachusetts Historical Society; Sean P. Casey, Cecile W. Gardner and especially Aaron Schmidt of the Boston Public Library; Pam Bennett and Laura Northridge of the Old North Foundation; Steven Greenberg of the Vilna Shul; Leah Cornwell of Lou Jones Studio; Katy Abel of the Boston Museum; and Arthur Felder III and Mary Luhrs of Corbis. I must also recognize Narine Dadayan, Brian Egan and Yohannes Endalew of the wonderfully hospitable Sheraton Commander Hotel in Cambridge for their help in photographing the old North End rooster.

For their comments and suggestions on the manuscript, I am indebted to Dr. Allan Cameron, Laura Cameron, Michael Chisholm, Priscilla Duffy, Sandi Orenstein, Charles Piccolo, Emily Piccolo, Vickie Stringfellow, Leah

Walczak and, of course, Mariel Gonzales. For editing the manuscript, preparing the index and offering expert advice, I heartily thank Julie Bogart. I also owe my gratitude to Dr. Timothy Hacsi of the University of Massachusetts Boston, who never seemed to doubt that I would publish my research on the North End. In addition, I thank Saunders Robinson of The History Press, not only for making this project possible, but for her enthusiastic efforts to make history accessible to the general public.

The sustained interest of so many members of my large family, including my late father, Charles Goldfeld, provided invaluable momentum during my long hours in reading rooms or in front of my computer. I also derived deep encouragement from my friends and neighbors in the North End who freely shared their memories of the neighborhood and trusted me to use them well.

A TOPPLED LANDMARK

Hurricane Carol assaulted the East Coast of the United States in August 1954 and crossed New England on the last day of the month. With drenching rains and sustained winds of 80 to 100 miles per hour and gusts of 100 to 130 miles per hour, the hurricane caused hundreds of millions of dollars worth of damage and dozens of deaths. Many North Enders today remember seeing the steeple of the Old North Church swaying during the storm on the morning of August 31. Reverend Charles Peck was the vicar of the church at that time, and he also saw the steeple moving back and forth in the terrible winds. It soon became clear that the steeple might actually be knocked down. Two Boston policemen began evacuating residents of Salem Street near the church, especially assisting the elderly.

The police told Reverend Peck and a handful of people gathered inside the church with him to leave, but they refused. Shortly before noon, after the church—and indeed the whole neighborhood—had endured the bulk of the storm, one final gust snapped the church's tower. For a moment, the white steeple, with its clock and ancient weather vane, was suspended in the air above Salem Street. Then the steeple came crashing down, and the majority of the impact was absorbed by the building at the corner of Salem and Hull Streets, which is still standing. The wooden steeple was smashed to pieces, and the brick church tower was cracked open. The skies began to clear as the storm moved out of Boston, and the historic steeple was now a pile of broken boards strewn across rooftops, dangling from fire escapes and obstructing the streets in front of the church. The eight massive bells were still hanging in the tower, as they had been since 1745, but they were now exposed to the elements and any passing seagull. A piece of American history was lost. Or was it?

Above: Hurricane Carol tears the Old North Church steeple from its tower on August 31, 1954. Amateur photographer Joseph Spallino, visiting from New York City, captured this image. *Courtesy of the Bostonian Society/Old State House, Boston Streets Photograph Collection, circa 1865–1999, and AP/Wide World Photos.*

Left: Old North Church wreckage after Hurricane Carol. Three North Enders appear at the right, including Johnny "Shoes" Cammarata in the foreground. *Courtesy of the Bostonian Society/Old State House, Boston Streets Photograph Collection, circa 1865–1999, and the* Boston Globe.

The famous Old North Church is the most heavily visited historic site in Boston's North End. It is known across the country as the place where, in 1775, Paul Revere's signal lanterns helped alarm the countryside that British soldiers were sailing from Boston to attack the Patriot stronghold at Concord. Very few people know, however, that the original steeple of the Old North Church, from which the lanterns shined, was knocked down in a hurricane twenty years after the Revolution. The church built a new steeple, though it was about twenty-five feet shorter than the first, and put it in place in 1806, complete with the original weather vane. The congregation installed a clock in the steeple in 1870, an addition that was fairly common for churches in those days. By the 100th anniversary of Revere's lanterns, the current steeple was similar to the historical one, but it was by no means a replica. It was that second steeple that was toppled by Hurricane Carol in 1954. The church

Christ Church ("Old North Church") in the late 1800s. *Courtesy of the Bostonian Society/Old State House, Boston Streets Photograph Collection, circa 1865–1999.*

quickly rebuilt it after an ingenious fundraising campaign, and it does resemble the original as closely as possible. However, since this is the third steeple, one that Paul Revere never used or even saw, is the Old North Church a fake?

Visitors to the Old North Church today are not at all disappointed to learn that they are looking at a historical facsimile. They are happy to know that the brick tower and sanctuary are still standing after 285 years, and the story behind the steeples only makes the site more interesting. The truth is that the fabric of any building will eventually deteriorate, and if parts of a historic structure cannot be saved, at least they can be rebuilt. Such was the case with the Old North Church, and anyone who sees the sun shining on the steeple and glittering on the old weather vane can more easily envision America's past. The neighborhood's long and rich history has given it a certain "power of place," and a visit to the North End offers an authentic chance to glimpse the lives and times of those who came before us. Everything described in the pages that follow embraces one characteristic above all else: it all happened in the North End, a neighborhood of historic events and common moments that form our shared heritage.

CHAPTER 1

THE NORTH END'S EARLIEST YEARS

A century before the Old North Church was built, the North End of Boston was a peninsula surrounded by the waters of the Charles River and Boston Harbor on the north, west and east. To the south, or southwest to be more exact, the North End was connected to the rest of town at about the intersection of Hanover and Blackstone Streets. Over time, and as land has been added to Boston, the border of the North End neighborhood has wandered, sometimes to the west and sometimes to the south. However, for anyone living there in the last half century, the demolition of buildings and the erection of the elevated expressway (the "Central Artery") in the late 1940s and early 1950s clearly demarcated the North End and cemented the current boundaries of the neighborhood. These boundaries are still the Charles River to the north and Boston Harbor to the east. The western border is North Washington Street. The southern border is Cross Street from North Washington to Atlantic Avenue and Christopher Columbus Park. The stories that follow in this and the successive chapters are part of the rich history of this relatively small area, beginning with the first English colonists.

The Puritans Arrive

John Winthrop, Boston's founder, led a fleet of eleven ships with seven hundred people from England in 1630. The emigrants, over a quarter of whom died during the perilous voyage across the Atlantic Ocean, intended to create a new religious commonwealth in North America. Their first stop in New England was Salem, where some of the passengers made their homes. The others sailed on and soon reached Charlestown. From there they went on to Watertown, Roxbury, Dorchester and other villages. Winthrop himself briefly considered staying in Charlestown, but he and fewer than two hundred others crossed the river to settle in Boston. Governor Winthrop landed in the North End, at the intersection of what would become Prince and Commercial Streets. Winthrop proceeded through the North End, which was at that time an open pasture with marshes and bushes, a small quantity of trees and an abundance of coastline along Boston's large harbor. The area to the south and west of Prince and Salem Streets was underwater, so the first settlers walked along the water's edge. The colonists eventually left the North End to settle around today's Old State House, which was in the center between the North and South Ends of colonial Boston.

Winthrop had thus learned that entering Boston was easiest and most efficient by taking a boat from one of the surrounding communities and landing in the North End. Boston in the 1600s was built on a peninsula with a very narrow connection to the mainland. The Back Bay, South End and Chinatown communities that we know today are built on filled mud flats, with the exception of Washington Street. Entering Boston by land in the earliest days, therefore, meant traveling on foot or by horse from any neighboring town through Roxbury and then up Washington Street to Boston. There were no bridges, no regular stagecoaches and very few roads. Traveling to and from Boston by boat was much faster, and the North End made the best geographical sense as a water-based transportation hub. Not only was the North End readily accessible from both the Charles River and Boston Harbor, but it was also physically closest to other areas of settlement just across the water, such as Charlestown, Chelsea, East Boston and Cambridge.

In 1631, the colonial government, under the leadership of Governor Winthrop, established the first regular ferry service in Massachusetts. The ferry ran between Charlestown and the North End, at Prince and Commercial Streets. A few years later, a second ferry was instituted from the North End, at Commercial and Hanover Streets, to Chelsea. Both ferries continued in service for over 150 years and brought thousands of settlers, visitors, traders and sailors to the North End, making it a very busy place. Boston's harbor was deep along the North End, and it could accommodate large sailing vessels. North Enders were especially industrious in building wharves on the North End's waterfront, which was more extensive than the original South End waterfront. During the colonial period, nearly everything east of North Street, from Battery Street to Blackstone Street, was underwater. North Street, therefore, was the coastline, and it was there that the earliest North Enders built their homes and their wharves. Colonial North Enders preferred to keep a close eye on their businesses, so the first houses in the

North End were built along North Street, directly across from the numerous wharves where boats docked to deliver people, products and news from the rest of the world. Individual lots of land along North Street often reached back to Hanover Street, which was not the main street that it is today.

Seventeenth-century North Enders considered North Street and the harbor to be the front of the neighborhood, Hanover Street was the middle and the Salem Street area, as well as Copp's Hill, with its nearby ferry traffic, formed the less desirable rear of the district. Copp's Hill was too steep and too far from the harbor to attract residents as quickly as the North Street area did. However, because it was close to the colony's first ferry service, it made an ideal location for the colony's first windmill. The windmill was originally located up the Charles River in Watertown. Unfortunately, the wind patterns there were not conducive to keeping the mill running at full capacity. The colonial government decided to move the windmill as early as 1632, and although there were many hills in Watertown, Charlestown, Roxbury and other places, the government chose Copp's Hill in the North End. Because residents of other towns would have to travel to this windmill until they had mills of their own, the most convenient location for the windmill was near the ferries and the river, where it could be approached by boat on a regular basis. The windmill, which ground corn and other grains into flour, became a vital part of food production in the young colony. For new immigrants and local travelers alike, Copp's Hill's grassy heights and the bobbing masts of the ships along North Street were the first signs that they had reached the bustling seaport of Boston.

Infrastructure of the Neighborhood

When Boston was founded, the North End was nearly an island, completely surrounded by water except for a constricted strip of land that connected it to the rest of the town. That strip of land was basically Hanover Street, leading north from Blackstone Street and spanning only as far as the marshy areas of North Street to the east and Salem Street to the west. Prior to the Revolution, this was the only way to enter the North End by land. In May 1643, Boston authorized the cutting of a creek to connect a western cove along the Charles River to the Town Cove, which is the area where Faneuil Hall would be built a century later. The creek was cut along the route of today's Blackstone Street, thus making an island of the North End. Later that summer, the town government granted the western cove bordered by North Margin Street to four individuals charged with the task of partially enclosing it—this would allow the flowing waters to run additional mills for the benefit of the town. From then on, this body of water would be known either as the Mill Cove or the Mill Pond, though it has since been filled in and built upon.

Boston's leaders then ordered the completion of fortifications near Boston Harbor, including the North Battery, which today is the site of new housing at Battery Wharf, at the end of Battery Street. The North Battery and all of the other fortifications were intended to help protect Boston Harbor from invading French or Dutch ships. However, no foreign nations were so bold as to directly attack Boston through its own harbor during the colonial period. Still, Bostonians considered the North Battery a necessary part of their defense, and they maintained it for generations. As construction began on the North Battery, early Bostonians also increased the number of streets, especially in the North End. North Street and Hanover Street are two of the oldest because they border the first areas of settlement in the North End. Other streets that connect these two, such as Cross, Richmond, Fleet and Battery, also date back to the first fifteen years of Boston's history. These are all part of the front of the North End.

The back of the North End had its own infrastructure in the earliest days of settlement. Parts of Prince, Commercial and Snowhill Streets are actually the oldest in the entire neighborhood. The need to reach the windmill necessitated the creation of Snowhill Street, and the fact that the ferries made this a major point of entry for Boston led to the creation of the surrounding streets. In 1643, the town government ordered the front and back of the North End to be physically connected by long, east–west roads. The result was the construction of Prince and Charter Streets, from Hanover all the way up to Commercial, "as directly as the land will beare." The selectmen knew that both roads would have to turn slightly at certain points to make the most convenient paths around Copp's Hill.

After the neighborhood was more coherently connected through its streets, the residents of the North End began to truly see themselves as inhabiting a distinct part of Boston. This sense of community came to the forefront in a set of "Proposicons presented to the Townsmen on the behalfe of the Inhabitants of the North End of the towne of Boston" in 1646. Because North Enders had already funded the construction of the North Battery, they believed that they should be free from taxes and assessments to build the other planned fortifications until such time as "the other part of the towne" contributed at least as much as they had. This petition is the earliest record of a growing consciousness among North Enders, as they began to develop a unique sense of place and community connection in the North End.

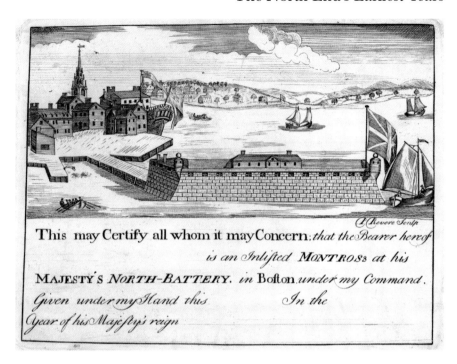

This may Certify all whom it may Concern: that the Bearer hereof is an Inlisted MONTROSS at his MAJESTY'S NORTH-BATTERY. in Boston under my Command. Given under my Hand this   In the Year of his Majesty's reign

A certificate for military service at the North Battery printed from an engraving by Paul Revere. This battery was originally built in the 1640s, but it is over a century old in Revere's depiction. The Old North Church tower is on the left, and Charlestown is in the background. *Courtesy of the Massachusetts Historical Society.*

Regular worship also enhanced community cohesion in the North End. Initially, North Enders attended Boston's only church, which was located in the South End. The original South End is known today as the Financial District and the Downtown Crossing shopping area. During the 1640s, in addition to church attendance, North Enders also conducted informal prayer meetings in local homes, and, in 1649, they officially formed a separate church. This was the first time that any town in the colony had established a second church. It not only reinforced the feeling of distinction, the sense that the North End was a neighborhood with its own characteristics, but it also indicated that the North End was populous and prosperous enough to support a separate church and minister.

CHAPTER 2

THE OLD NORTH MEETING HOUSE

The Center of the Community

Since the Puritans had been persecuted in England for their religious practices, they were defensive of their Congregationalism in America. Unfortunately, their defensiveness quickly became institutionalized intolerance in colonial Massachusetts. In a society founded specifically as a place to cultivate only one expression of Christianity, churches naturally became places of power and influence. Although all Bostonians were required to attend church services, which they called "meetings," church membership requirements were so difficult that only about 10 percent of the people in church every Sunday were full members. Consequently, these people owned most of the property, held most of the public offices and generally made most of the decisions in the public sphere. When North Enders opened their own church, they effectively created a power node in Boston that might one day grow stronger than that of the South End, which in 1649 contained the only church, as well as the town hall and school.

It should be noted that early Bostonians did not refer to their religious buildings as "churches." They almost always called them "meeting houses." Avoiding the word "church" had specific meaning for the early Puritans. For them, "church" referred to the body of members, not the building. In addition, the term was usually used in reference to the Church of England, and New England meetinghouses were deliberately created as the antitheses of the Anglican churches. The original Bostonians were also careful to avoid any confusion between their Congregationalism and the Roman Catholic Church. New England towns also had schoolhouses, jailhouses, town houses and, on the coast, lighthouses, among others. The Puritans' fascination with the ancient Hebrews was another reason that they continued to use meetinghouses, schoolhouses and the like. In the Hebrew language, a school, for example, is called a *bet sefer*—literally "book house." This was also consistent with the Puritans' proclivity for assigning the simplest names possible to public buildings and notable aspects of the landscape.

Boston's new meetinghouse was ready for occupancy in the spring of 1650. Because there was only one other meetinghouse in town, this one was sometimes referred to as the "new meeting house" but most often was called the North Meeting House. Its construction directly led to the creation of a public square in the North End. Bell Alley (now mostly part of Prince Street) and Sun Court, Garden Court and Moon Streets were laid out along with the North Meeting House, and the area known today as North Square was established.

The North End continued to grow throughout the mid-seventeenth century, and new homes, wharves and streets were established along the waterfront. Various types of taverns, with licenses to sell food, coffee, beer, liquor or even chocolate drinks, opened in North Square and along North Street. The first was a "house of common entertainment," run by John Vyall and James Davis in 1652 near the North Meeting House. In barely more than a decade after the North Meeting House opened, proprietors established several other taverns in the area, including the Red Lion Inn at the corner of North and Richmond Streets; the Salutation Inn, located on Salutation Street, close to North Street; and the Ship Tavern on North Street, between Fleet and Clark Streets. The North Meeting House and its congregation played a large role in generating community development.

The "Never-To-Be-Forgotten *Increase*"

The original North End congregation was small and independent, and its members were accustomed to lay people leading their meetings. One member in particular, Michael Powell, often led prayers and even preached, and the congregation proposed ordaining him as its minister in 1653. Although it was within the rights of individual congregations to ordain their own ministers, the other New England clergymen, as well as their allies in the colonial government, objected to the ordination of this uneducated man. The North Enders pleaded their case before the government and lost. Over the objections of Powell and many in his community, an established minister, educated and bourgeois, was installed in the North End. John Mayo, who had been living in the Plymouth Colony since 1639, became the first ordained minister of the North End. For over fifteen years, he had ministered in Barnstable and Eastham on Cape Cod. Despite its objections to the new minister, the congregation at the North Meeting House continued to grow because avoiding meetings was simply not an option.

In 1664, Increase Mather was ordained as "teacher" to assist John Mayo at the North Meeting House in a ceremony conducted by Mayo and Increase's aged father, Richard Mather. Increase was twenty-five years old at the time, but because of his interpretation of scriptures and his impressive preaching skills, it wasn't long before he became the senior minister. The dynamic young cleric was born in the town of Dorchester, and his father was one of the leading clergymen in all of New England. According to a family story, Richard named his son in honor of the "never-to-be-forgotten *Increase*, of every sort, where with GOD favored the Country, about the time of his Nativity." When Increase Mather accepted the position at the North Meeting House, a controversy was brewing among all of the church members in Boston and the surrounding towns. Certain ministers wanted to relax the requirements for church membership, but the bulk of existing church members strongly opposed these suggested changes because they had already passed the earlier, more stringent tests of faith. Mather publicly opposed changing the rules, a stance that won him a great deal of popularity among church members in the North End and elsewhere.

The North End's only congregation was poised to become the most powerful in Boston. The majority of ministers, including very prominent men like Increase's father, eventually voted to support individual congregations that wished to loosen their membership rules. The controversy surrounding this decision created simmering divisions within Boston's First Meeting House, a congregation that did not adopt the practice. A new congregation split from the first, becoming the Third Meeting House in Boston (today's Old South Church in Copley Square). Because the Third congregation was newly established and followed more liberal rules, and the First congregation was divided and weakened, the North End congregation now had the opportunity to rise in prominence. Under the vigorous direction of Increase Mather, whose popularity had only increased during the controversy, the North Meeting House retained a large membership and became the town's leading religious institution.

After Mayo's departure in 1673, Mather became the senior minister of the church, more immersed than ever in his work to save the souls of every North Ender. He published his fiery sermons and began writing books on various religious topics, all of which served to spread his holy message and cement his position as the leading Puritan minister in the colony. Mather became a very powerful man, and prosperous people moved to the North End to be closer to him and his congregation. Because of its busy water traffic, the neighborhood was already filled with visitors and bustling with commercial activity, but Mather's strong leadership turned the neighborhood

Increase Mather (1639–1723) of Hanover Street, 1688. *Courtesy of the Massachusetts Historical Society.*

into the religious focal point of the town. In Massachusetts society, religious prominence meant political power. By the 1670s, the North End was Boston's premier address.

A Series of Disasters

A number of unfortunate events in the mid-1670s tested the faith of Increase Mather and his congregation and simultaneously led to a sizable increase in the number of people and diversity of opinions within the North End. The English people and Native Americans of New England had maintained a relatively peaceful coexistence since the end of the Pequot War in 1637. Forty years later, most Bostonians feared a coastal attack from Dutch enemies of England more than they did an uprising of native peoples from the interior of the colony. The fear of attack from other nations was a palpable part of life throughout Boston and the colony. Fearing a European attack, the people of Massachusetts did not expect a war with Native Americans in 1675. However, a coalition of Wampanoags, Nipmucks and Narragansetts, under the leadership of Metacomet, or "King Philip," began attacking English settlements that summer.

Soon, all of New England was at war. At first, North End residents and merchants were insulated from the war. Most of the attacks occurred in the rural communities, and the fighting did not seriously disrupt seaborne commerce. Yet, King Philip's forces partially or totally burned Lancaster, Medfield, Groton, Marlborough and other villages. As they drew closer to Boston with attacks on Billerica and Woburn, English refugees streamed into the capital for protection. Despite the fact that many of the native peoples had adopted their religion and converted to Christianity, the English came to see all Native Americans as their enemies. Though King Philip was assassinated in the summer of 1676, thus ending the war, confusion and sorrow spread across the North End as survivors grappled with moving forward. A few months later, however, further devastation struck the small neighborhood.

On November 27, 1676, a fire began in the vicinity of the Red Lion Inn. Most homes and taverns burned small, controlled fires all the time for light, heat and cooking. The potential for these flames to spread out of control, combined with the general use of wood in the construction of the majority of buildings, left the North End at constant risk of burning to the ground. That is what happened on that November morning when a tailor's assistant rose very early to begin his day's work. He fell asleep, and his light began to burn the materials in the shop. The fire grew, spread and destroyed nearly everything in North Square, including the North Meeting House and the home of Increase Mather. In the predawn hours, the entire Mather family escaped the flames that took their house. But Increase tried to save his impressive library by running back into the house with his nephew,

The Mather-Eliot House, circa 1899. Increase Mather and his family moved into this house in 1677. In the eighteenth century, the building became home to Reverend Andrew Eliot. A tablet was placed on the building in 1907 to commemorate its historical significance, but the building was demolished a few years later. On the site today is the White Hen Pantry at 342 Hanover Street. *Courtesy of the Bostonian Society/Old State House, Boston Streets Photograph Collection, circa 1865–1999.*

John, and son, Cotton, then only thirteen years old. They grabbed as many books and manuscripts as they could and piled them into the street, where it was raining. Without a fire department, and in spite of the rain, the fire continued into the daylight. North Enders could only stand and watch as some of their neighbors blew up buildings to stop the spread of the fire. Between the spectacular explosions and the fire itself, nearly fifty buildings were destroyed.

A town meeting previously scheduled for that night was canceled because of "ye sad desolation by fire at the North end of ye Towne." In December and January, five town meetings subsequently followed. A group of men was appointed and tasked with inspecting chimneys and enforcing all existing fire regulations; thus, Boston's earliest version of a fire department stemmed from a North End tragedy. In addition, the selectmen ordered that no one could build anything in the destroyed area until the streets were re-laid out. Over the next few years, North Enders applied for reimbursement, not only for buildings deliberately destroyed in the path of the fire, but also for powder used to create the explosions. The North Meeting House was quickly rebuilt, but the Mathers moved to a house on Hanover Street. Their move may have been prompted by the restriction on new buildings in the ruined North Square.

The town finished laying out the streets in the burned area that were "wider and more acomodable to the publique" in the summer of the following year. New buildings were slowly constructed, some unwisely of wood, including one home that survives to this day as the only seventeenth-century structure in the North End. This is "Paul Revere's House," built circa 1680 on the site of the Mathers' home. Although the center of the neighborhood was destroyed, the wharves and warehouses survived the blaze. Trade with other ports and investments in ships allowed North Enders to rebuild their neighborhood more quickly and thoroughly than the less fortunate colonists in rural Massachusetts. Sadly, the tribulations of North Enders and their fellow Bostonians were not over. In 1678, a smallpox epidemic tore through the town. There was no known cure for this quick and deadly disease, and the North End was especially at risk whenever a new ship came into port. The disease ran its course, but the North End was faced with new dangers in the years that followed, from political as well as supernatural forces.

The North Meeting House and the Massachusetts Bay Colony

In 1688, Increase and Cotton Mather, two of the most well-known North Enders of their day, played a role in the colony-wide controversies concerning the Massachusetts Bay charter and the infiltration of the colony by witches. Cotton, Increase Mather's eldest child, had been ordained as a co-minister with his father at the North Meeting House in 1684. Because the North Meeting House gave them such a prominent platform, both Mathers were able to frequently express their ideas and utilize their unique talents. The Massachusetts charter allowed the colony to govern itself in practice, though it was still a colony of the Kingdom of England. By the early 1680s, London wanted to assert greater control over colonial affairs from Maine to the Caribbean so as to smooth out differences, increase efficiency and obtain a larger piece of the profits from international trade. Massachusetts was asked to surrender its charter so that necessary adjustments could be made.

North Enders, just like others across Massachusetts, voted overwhelmingly not to surrender the charter. The king responded by simply revoking it. For over fifty years, the charter had been the legal basis for life in Massachusetts. Bostonians' interpretation of the charter—and the freedoms it guaranteed—had allowed them to ignore certain economic and religious restrictions, earning the ire of the king and Parliament. In fact, Bostonians were used to breaking laws, especially if they could avoid customs inspections or paying taxes to London. After their cherished charter was revoked, the colonial government decided to send one person to London to represent all of Massachusetts. They chose one of the most respected, articulate, powerful and politically astute men in the colonies: Increase Mather.

Mather sailed for England in 1688. After four years of negotiations with two different kings, dozens of government ministers and private citizens sympathetic to the cause of Massachusetts, Mather succeeded in obtaining a new charter that retained many of the same rights as the original. However, under the new charter, the governor was to be appointed by the Crown and no longer elected by the people. The Governor's Council members, the upper house of the legislature, were nominated by the lower house but had to be approved by the royal governor. The representatives in the lower house were to be elected by the freeholders, but voters no longer needed to be church members as specified under the old charter. In addition, the Massachusetts Bay Colony was re-created into the Province of Massachusetts Bay, and Plymouth Colony, Nantucket Island and Maine all became part of the new province.

William Phips (1651–1695) of Charter Street, circa 1692. *Courtesy of the Commonwealth of Massachusetts, Art Commission.*

Mather was asked to recommend an individual to be the first governor under the new charter, and he nominated another North End resident, Sir William Phips. A native of Maine, now incorporated with Massachusetts, Phips had distinguished himself as a sailor, warrior and adventurer and had previously been knighted for generously sharing some of the treasure he had found with the king. Due to the involvement of Mather and Phips, North Enders were heavily represented on the new Governor's Council. This alienated South Enders, who refused to elect any North Enders to high offices in Boston for over fifteen years. But Mather's personal popularity remained high. Harvard College awarded Mather a doctoral degree in theology, the first ever awarded in America, and Dr. Mather served as the first native-born president of the college until 1701. Unfortunately, Phips was temperamentally better suited to war and life at sea than to politics. His public support quickly diminished in Massachusetts, and he was recalled to London to answer allegations of misuse of his power after only two years. His case was never heard because he died soon after his arrival in England.

Back in the summer of 1688, shortly after Increase Mather had sailed for England to fight for the charter, four children in the South End home of John Goodwin were "visited with strange Fits, beyond those that attend an Epilepsy." Martha, the eldest of the afflicted children, was thirteen at the time. Apparently, her seizures and strange behavior began when she was scolded by Ann Glover. Martha Goodwin had accused the family's laundress, Mrs. Glover's daughter, of stealing linens. Mrs. Glover rebuked young Goodwin for her baseless accusation, and the teenager in turn accused Glover of being a witch. The Goodwin children continued their fantastic behavior, and Glover was put on trial to determine whether she was really the supernatural cause of their anguish. Glover's daughter was not charged with theft, and the linens were later found in the Goodwin household. The possibility that Ann Glover, whom Cotton Mather described as a "Hag" and "an ignorant and a scandalous old Woman," was a real witch truly concerned the ministers and civil authorities.

Glover was indeed convicted of being a witch and was hanged on Boston Common in November 1688. The American-Irish Historical Society, writing about the incident in 1905, stated that the people of Massachusetts were "saturated with prejudice," that the "trial of Mrs. Glover was a farce" and that she was "put to death not so much because she was reputed a witch, as for the certainty that she was a Catholic." Ann Glover, who is remembered today as "Goody Glover," was from Ireland. She spoke mostly in Gaelic, she recited the Lord's Prayer in Latin and, much to the consternation of Cotton Mather, she was a devout "Roman Catholick." Glover had lived in Boston for several years before her execution, and her Catholicism was a constant irritant to the Puritans. Cotton Mather detested Catholics, a popular attitude that played a very large role in Glover's death, but he also really believed in witches and sought to perfect the methodology for discovering them. He published two influential books on the subject between 1689 and 1692 and immediately became involved in the allegations of witchcraft in Salem Village during that time. Indeed, Mather's books on how to find witches may have exacerbated the situation in Salem. Governor Phips established a court to investigate the accusations and try the accused, nineteen of whom were executed. Mather publicly supported the trials because "it becomes the Embassadors of the L[ord] Jesus to leave no stroke untouch't that may conduce to bring men from the power of Satan unto God." Phips brought the trials to an end, however, when his wife was accused of witchcraft. As the seventeenth century came to a close, life in eastern Massachusetts finally began to return to normal, and the North End remained busy, prosperous and influential in local and provincial affairs.

"Old North"

Increase Mather continued his ministry at the North Meeting House until his death in 1723 at the remarkable age of eighty-four. Although his personal prestige was greatly magnified by his London mission, the relative power of Mather, like other Puritan ministers, slowly diminished in the early eighteenth century. Even with the backing of the government, Mather had been unable to disband the despised Baptist congregation that had settled in the North End in 1679. Ironically, the new charter he brokered in 1692 also weakened Puritan control of Massachusetts because it extended the limited franchise to members of other Christian denominations and to more of the landowners. In 1714, Increase and Cotton couldn't stop part of their congregation from leaving the North Meeting House. This new group established the second Congregational meetinghouse in the North End, on Hanover Street between Clark and Harris. In reference to the Mathers' building, the new congregation built the New North Meeting House, or "New North" for short. The meetinghouse in North Square was known as "Old North" until its destruction by occupying British soldiers in 1776.

CHAPTER 3

AFRICAN AMERICANS IN THE NORTH END

The history of African Americans in the North End is the story of both free and enslaved Africans and their descendants. Some North Enders, like other white people across New England, held Africans and Native Americans in bondage in the 1600s and 1700s. Purchasing human beings, even if you had to split the cost with a relative or business partner, was considered a good investment. At the time of her death, even Paul Revere's maternal grandmother owned a part of a black man named Nulgar. Slavery developed differently in each colony, but Massachusetts was an early leader in the practice. Massachusetts merchants brought the first enslaved Africans to Boston in February 1638 with the goal of increasing the economic competitiveness in the young settlement. Native Americans were increasingly deemed "very ungovernable" as slaves because of their relatives and allies in the region. However, any natives captured in "just warres," according to law, could be treated as slaves, which meant that they could be traded for Africans. Because African slaves worked for free and had few rights, they were also a better investment than white indentured servants.

Free Black North Enders

By the 1650s, because slavery was not necessarily for life in Massachusetts, free black people lived in the area. The North End was still a very small community in the 1650s, and there were probably very few black people in the neighborhood. In fact, there were only about two thousand people in all of Boston. As the 1600s progressed, however, the overall population of Boston grew, including the number of black people. A small number of free African Americans began to settle near one another on Copp's Hill, close to the intersection of Charter and Snowhill Streets. Bostonians, like people in other communities, only allowed black people to live on the least desirable land. In colonial Boston, this meant areas not only on hills, but also near proto-industrial land uses. Copp's Hill was considered to be the rear of the North End, and white North Enders settled it last because of its steepness and because of the windmill, busy ferry traffic and the distance from North Street. It was there that the small free community lived, along with some enslaved people not required to live in their enslavers' houses. In 1659, the town had opened a cemetery on Copp's Hill, adjacent to the black community, and it is there that the earliest black North Enders found their final resting place. A handful of tombstones can still be seen over the graves of African Americans on Copp's Hill, but the majority were stolen or destroyed long ago.

Free African Americans found work in the wind- and water mills near their homes. A variety of mills were built on the Mill Pond, and its waters

Copp's Hill Burying Ground. Most black Bostonians from the seventeenth and eighteenth centuries are buried in this area of the North End's cemetery. The intersection beyond the tree is Charter and Snowhill Streets.

were the repository for mill-related waste products, such as the organs of animals whose skins were used for leather or the yeasty remains from the brewing process. Since 1679, the First Baptist Church was also located on the pond, where it was shunned by the dominant Puritans of the North Meeting House. According to historical archaeologist Cheryl LaRoche, early African Americans were often attracted to adult baptism as a way to re-humanize themselves after (or during) their experiences in slavery. Colonial black settlements could often be found near a Baptist church. The First Baptist Church would count some of the leading black Bostonians among its parishioners in the next century.

In the 1600s, everyone in Boston was expected to be at services at one of the Puritan meetinghouses on Sunday, even if they were not eligible for full membership. Because of this, black North Enders attended services at the North Meeting House, but local African Americans also worshiped on their own, often in the home of a community leader. African and European traditions led to the development of distinctly different styles of preaching, modes of personal expression and even the types of music played in black and white churches. African-American religious services were further influenced by the general experience of slavery and the hope of deliverance in Massachusetts and across the country. These circumstances motivated many black people to participate in prayer meetings that did not include white Bostonians.

The First Black Church in Boston

In 1693, Cotton Mather attended a black prayer meeting in the North End. According to his diary in 1684, the year of his ordination at the North Meeting House, Mather had resolved to say silent prayers for people he passed on the streets. For example, if he saw a group of children playing, he would say (to himself), "Lord, help these Persons to remember their Creator in the Dayes of their Youth." If he passed a local merchant, he would say, "Lord, make that man a wise merchant." However, if he passed a black person, he would say, "Lord, wash that poor Soul white in the Blood of thy Son." Unfortunately, Mather's worldview caused him to conflate slavery and Christianity, and he brought his views with him to the African-American prayer meeting.

Mather wrote that he was invited to the prayer meeting, possibly for his knowledge of scriptures, but most likely for the legitimacy and protection his approval of the services would confer. Based on his experience with African

Americans in the North End that night, he published *Rules for the Society of Negroes*. It was a list of eight rules of conduct, later extended to nine, for the "Miserable Children of Adam, and of Noah…[who] freely Resolve…to become the Servants" of God and the Lord Jesus Christ, and "in the Service of our Heavenly Master, we now Join together in a SOCIETY, wherein the following RULES are to be observed." The incorporated churches of Boston were known as religious "societies," and although this group of black people was not legally incorporated as a formal church and did not have a church building of its own, this "Society of Negroes" in the North End is the earliest known African-American religious community in Boston.

Unfortunately, but not altogether unexpectedly, the *Rules* of 1693 had as much to do with maintaining slavery as promoting Christianity. Mather encouraged observing the Sabbath, avoiding wicked or sinful people and abstaining from drunkenness, swearing, lying and fornication. He also reserved for himself the right to approve or deny adding additional members to the society. In addition, Mather wrote that attendance at services was dependent on the consent of "such as have Power over us"—a clear reference to one's master or enslaver. Members of the society were also to report any African Americans who were out of doors in the evening without a pass, and they were strictly admonished not to provide shelter to fugitives. Mather would expel from the society anyone found guilty of harboring an escaped slave.

The Case of Adam Saffin

About seven thousand people lived in Boston in 1692, when Increase Mather and William Phips brought the new charter back from London. Over the next thirty-five years, the population of the town doubled, including the number of enslaved and free Africans. The closer relationship with the royal government in England brought a whole new class of royal appointees to Boston, particularly in the North End. Changes in English law in 1696 allowed all Englishmen to legally engage in the slave trade, causing a surge in that peculiar type of commerce. According to legal historian Leon Higginbotham, by the 1700s, New England was the "most active slave-trading area in America." Trading and investing in African people not only added to the small population of black people in Boston but also brought great wealth to the town. The increasing number of African Americans in Massachusetts, as well as the spread of slavery, caused a heated argument between John Saffin, a Massachusetts judge, and Adam Saffin, a man whose term of enslavement to John had ended. Apparently, John had rented Adam to a man working on one of his farms in Bristol in 1694. The contract stated that if Adam worked faithfully and industriously for seven years, John would "make free my said negro man Adam to be fully at his own Dispose and Liberty as other free men are."

In 1701, believing that he was free, Adam traveled to Boston. John ordered him to return to Bristol, but Adam stayed in Boston, most likely in the North End. John traveled to Boston to settle the matter, but fellow judge Samuel Sewall, who owned land next to the black settlement on Copp's Hill, subpoenaed John to appear in court. Less than a year prior to this incident, Sewall had published a pamphlet entitled *The Selling of Joseph: A Memorial*. In it Sewall argued that all people were created by God and have an equal right to liberty; slavery, he wrote, was not a natural condition. Sewall encouraged the end of African slavery and the development of indentured servitude of white people. This attitude was contrary to popular opinion and economic theory. Sewall enthusiastically took up the case of Adam Saffin, which lasted for over two years. In the end, Adam won his freedom, and he remained in Boston.

The issue of slavery and the rights of African Americans did not disappear, however. In May 1701, the selectmen of Boston echoed Sewall's argument by urging their representatives in the government of Massachusetts to encourage the expansion of white servitude and "to put a Period to negros being Slaves." The government responded by issuing a series of laws that raised the importation tax on each enslaved black person, while awarding a cash bonus for each male white servant between the ages of eight and twenty-five brought into Massachusetts. As usual, Bostonians became adept at avoiding the new taxes through smuggling. Sexual relations and marriage between white ("any person of the English or other Christian nation") and black people were strictly forbidden. A curfew of 9:00 p.m. was imposed on enslaved black people (and Native Americans). Constables, watchmen, justices of the peace and just about any white landowner had the power to "take up and apprehend" anyone breaking curfew. Adam Saffin, even after obtaining his freedom, could be questioned or harassed by any white person on the streets of the North End, even children, and could be held against his will or imprisoned for being outside after 9:00 p.m. Saffin and other free black North Enders enjoyed a very restricted type of freedom.

Public Works and the Charity School

African Americans and Native Americans were exempt from military service in Massachusetts, but so were various church leaders, Harvard personnel,

Samuel Sewall (1652–1730) in 1728. *Courtesy of the Massachusetts Historical Society.*

people in essential positions like constant ferrymen and some millworkers, and most of the legislators. Because of their exemption from military duty, a 1707 act "regulating" free African Americans required those of able body to repair and clean the streets of each town, at the discretion of the local selectmen. None of the exempt white people were required to report for this or any other sort of replacement service. From 1708 through 1725, and sporadically thereafter, the selectmen of Boston regularly assembled the *free* black men to service the streets. These men, during that time period, collectively performed an average of 149 days of unpaid work each year.

Adam Saffin, who had endured slavery and fought for his own right to be free, found himself on the work list continually between 1708 and 1715. The surnames of other African Americans summoned for service, like Phillip Hutchinson, Dick Dudley, Mingo Winthrop, Exeter Foxcroft and Onesimus Mather, revealed the prominent citizens, including clergymen, who practiced slavery. The street cleaning law did not affect enslaved people because their enslavers would lose work and income if their slaves were busy working for the town instead. Free African Americans forced to work in the streets without compensation, on the other hand, could otherwise be working to earn money for themselves and their families. Thus, the Massachusetts government ingeniously extended the effects of slavery into the lives of free people in the North End and elsewhere for its own economic benefit. In defending Adam Saffin and promoting an end to African slavery, Samuel Sewall truly held a minority view.

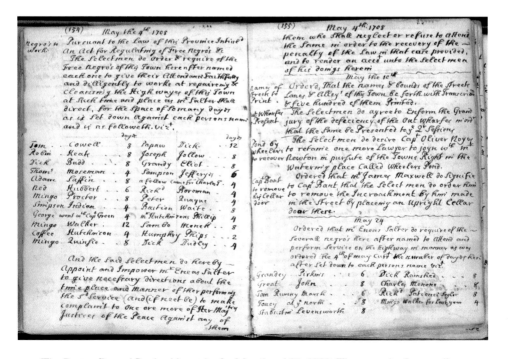

The Boston Record Book with entries for May 4 and 24, 1708. These are the first two lists of men called to service in Boston under the 1707 provincial law. Adam Saffin is the fifth person listed. *Courtesy of the Boston Public Library, Department of Rare Books & Manuscripts.*

During the first half of the eighteenth century, the North End underwent a period of growth, aided by Adam Saffin and the other unpaid laborers. It was during that time that the selectmen formally established two public schools in the North End. Unfortunately, African Americans, even those who were free, were not welcomed at these schools. The distinction between "public" and "private" schools was not as clear then as it is today. All schools received tax money and, at the same time, charged the parents of students a variety of fees for educational services. Because access to the North End's schools required private payments, the churches asked for donations to run "charity schools" for the poorest residents. When a charity school opened in the North End in 1710, Cotton Mather noted that it was filled beyond capacity by 1713, indicating the growing complexity of North End society. As one of the most famous North Enders of his day and a strong advocate of charity schools, Mather paid all of the expenses for a charity school for African Americans and Native Americans between 1718 and 1721. He funded the instruction of Bible and catechism reading but did not support writing instruction at his charity school.

Mather did believe in the immortal souls of people of color, prompting his interest in teaching them to read the Bible. However, he personally practiced slavery and even wrote a guide for other white people on how to properly educate slaves about Christianity. Published in 1706, Mather's book *The Negro Christianized* encouraged black people to think of their enslavers in the same way they would Jesus Christ. He instructed white people to lead African Americans in the recitation of the following prayer, among others: "My Saviour shall be my Master; He is a Good Master; He has Bought me to Serve Him; and He will make me a Child of God." Although it is notable that Cotton Mather tried to provide charity for African Americans, his dedication to saving the souls of black people was always shadowed by his negative attitudes toward what he called the "black sheep in my flock." Massachusetts was a slave society, and Mather's attitudes were not uncommon at all. Even Samuel Sewall, who had advocated for the end of slavery both generally and specifically (as in the case of Adam Saffin), held negative attitudes about Africans. For example, about a decade after the Saffin case, Sewall openly discussed his conviction that black people would probably be white after the Second Coming of Jesus and the establishment of paradise on Earth.

More than a century after Cotton Mather opened a school for people of color, Boston's public schools remained segregated, and African-American boys and girls living in the North End had to leave the neighborhood for education. Rather than attending the local Eliot, Hancock or Endicott Schools, they walked to the Smith School on Joy Street, Beacon Hill, pictured here in 1849. The Smith School is now a museum. *Private collection.*

Onesimus Mather and Smallpox Inoculation

In April 1721, smallpox once again surfaced in Boston, brought by sailors on the *Seahorse*, a ship recently arrived from the West Indies. Not only did this deadly disease spread quickly, but there was also still no known cure. Bostonians tried to isolate the disease by communicating new instances of infection and placing those affected under quarantine. The selectmen ordered the cleansing of the streets to prevent the smallpox from spreading through town. Because this was dirty and dangerous work, twenty-six free black men had to work six days each, cleaning the streets and removing all dirt and debris. Luckily, many, if not all, of these men may have been immune to the smallpox due to a method of inoculating against the disease practiced in various parts of Africa. This procedure entailed placing some of the material from the inside of the sores of an infected person into a small cut in a healthy person. The healthy person would become sick, but usually only very mildly, then regain health without the threat of death. Once inoculated, a person was immune to future infections. Immune to the disease after contracting it during the outbreak of 1678, Cotton Mather once again created controversy.

Mather was a fellow of the Royal Society, a London-based organization dedicated to science. The Royal Society had researched the inoculation method as practiced in other parts of the world and published its findings. Cotton read the report and double-checked its facts with Onesimus, one of the people he enslaved. Back in 1706, Mather had been interested in purchasing a slave "at the expence of between forty and fifty pounds." Some members of the North Meeting House knew about his desire and purchased a young man for him on December 13. Mather named the young man Onesimus, though he surely already had a name of his own. Cotton noted that Onesimus knew how to read, and he considered teaching him how to write. Over the next ten years, however, Cotton felt that Onesimus became increasingly rebellious, and Cotton decided to allow him to purchase his

The Boston Record Book with entries for May 24 and June 5, 1721. The black men listed were each ordered to work six days cleaning the streets during the smallpox epidemic. *Courtesy of the Boston Public Library, Department of Rare Books & Manuscripts.*

own freedom. The money that Onesimus paid for himself was used to purchase a black boy as a replacement slave. Onesimus's freedom was not unconditional, however, and he still had to perform daily chores at Cotton's home on Hanover Street. He had to arrive with a shovel during "great snows," as well as generally help the Mather family by bringing grains to the mill on Copp's Hill, piling wood, fetching water and doing other tasks, whenever needed.

In 1721, Onesimus assured Cotton that inoculation was successfully practiced in Africa. Although many Bostonians believed that it was sinful and reckless to purposely infect healthy people with a deadly disease, Cotton was convinced that it would work. He circulated his own pamphlet on the topic among the physicians in Boston in June, but despite his efforts, they were violently opposed to the method. Only one person, Zabdiel Boylston, was receptive to Cotton's arguments. Disregarding threats and ridicule, Dr. Boylston visited African Americans around the town, all of whom generally confirmed their knowledge of the practice and its success in Africa. Boylston then inoculated his own son, as well as his enslaved man Jack and Jack's child. Between the springs of 1721 and 1722, nearly half of Boston's population became infected with smallpox and about 15 percent died. Boylston inoculated about 250 people, only six of whom met an unfortunate end. This provided the doctor with enough medical data to travel to London, where far fewer people had been inoculated. His practical experience helped validate the procedure for people living in England, and he was made a fellow of the Royal Society a few years after the crisis. Thus, Cotton, Onesimus and other North Enders helped make inoculation a reality in Boston as well as in London.

New Guinea

No contemporary records attribute any name to the African-American community on Copp's Hill. By the late nineteenth century, however, histories of the area began to refer to that part of the North End as "New Guinea," even though the community had moved to Beacon Hill decades before. It is also unclear if the name was derisively imposed on the black community by white Bostonians or if it originated with African Americans. According to sociologist and historian Adelaide Cromwell, it is nearly impossible to know exactly when or how a term such as "New Guinea" was first used, though it is probable that this particular term was first used by the white community in a negative way. "New Guinea" was later adopted

The Prince Hall Monument, circa 1900. Prince Hall (1735–1807) was a leader of Boston's black community during the Revolution and the founder of black Freemasonry in the United States. His grave on the Snowhill Street side of Copp's Hill Burying Ground is a reminder of the early black settlement in the North End. *Courtesy of the Museum of African American History, Boston, Massachusetts.*

The Boston Record Book with an entry for September 13, 1738. Onesimus Mather, who purchased his freedom twenty-two years earlier, is second on the work list. *Courtesy of the Boston Public Library, Department of Rare Books & Manuscripts.*

by the black community and, by the early twentieth century, had completely lost its derogatory connotations. One is reminded of the similar process concerning the term "Yankee," which was originally used by the English to mock colonial Americans.

It is not surprising that Boston's New Guinea is not marked on any map or prominently included in any early histories—such places often aren't. What is clear is that Africans and their descendants made their homes on the streets of the North End. Most local African Americans were held in slavery at some point, and all were subjected to the harsh laws of Massachusetts. They founded their own church in 1693, and it thrived as late as 1718—probably in part because Cotton Mather sanctioned the church, most likely supporting it until his death in 1728. Black North Enders allowed their children to attend Mather's private charity school, and one can safely assume that these parents sought other ways to educate their children during the decades in which they were excluded from the North End's public schools.

Boston's selectmen continued to force Onesimus and others to work in the streets, slowly stripping personal liberties away from African Americans. In the summer of 1728, for example, the selectmen forbid black people to carry sticks, canes or anything "fit for Quarreling," unless the accused person could absolutely prove that he was "Lame or Decriped." Yet, by 1730, African Americans had helped build Boston into the largest town in British North America, with the North End at the center of this prosperity and fashion.

CHAPTER 4

CENTENNIAL

The oldest surviving map of Boston dates to 1722, drawn by navigator and shipwright John Bonner. It is an accurate depiction of Boston as it reached its 100th birthday in 1730, when it was the largest town in the colonies and the North End was its most populous and desirable neighborhood. The first thing one should notice when looking at this map is the shape of the town of Boston. On the left side of the map is a narrow strip of land, the "neck," which connected Boston to the mainland at Roxbury. Following that strip farther onto the peninsula, one can see Boston Common clearly marked. Near the common is Beacon Hill, with an illustration of the emergency beacon atop a pole. This whole area of the map is light compared to the darker parts lower on the map. The dark marks represent buildings, and the darkest areas represent the most densely populated sections of town. Clearly, most Bostonians, after a century of settlement, still lived along the part of the peninsula closest to Boston Harbor.

On the map, Long Wharf, completed in 1710, extends from the center of town out into the harbor, past all of the other wharves. To the left of this landmark on the map lies the original South End, which, in 1722, still housed a lot of open space. The North End, on the other hand—especially the area of land that stretched from the numerous wharves on the harbor to Salem Street—was the busiest and most built-up part of town. Besides the schools and churches in the neighborhood, other North End landmarks noted on Bonner's map include the North Battery, the windmill, the Charlestown ferry, the North Water Mill and the Burying Place on Copp's Hill. North Square ("Clark's Square") was just a block away from the water, and Clark's Wharf was clearly the largest and most prominent in the neighborhood. As a shipwright, Bonner was particularly sensitive to marking wharves and shipyards on his map. He shows us only one shipyard in the South End,

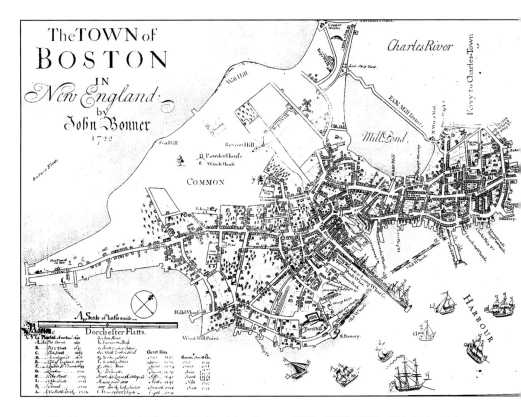

The Town of Boston in New England by John Bonner (1643–1726), 1722. This is the oldest surviving map of Boston. *Courtesy of the I.N. Phelps Stokes Collection, Miriam and Ira D. Wallach Division of Art, Prints and Photographs, the New York Public Library, Astor, Lenox and Tilden Foundations.*

along with barely more than a dozen wharves. By contrast, the North End has twice as many wharves and nine shipyards.

The Great Fire of 1711 temporarily halted the growth of the center and South End of Boston, indirectly contributing to further expansion in the North End. Shortly after the fire, wealthy families and the increasingly affluent merchant and artisan population in the North End built several large mansions and brick homes near North Square. The artisans, known then as "mechanics," were silversmiths, cobblers, tailors, sailmakers and shipwrights. "[F]ourteen substantial mechanics" founded and built New North on Hanover Street in 1714, and the rising prosperity of the neighborhood led to the establishment of the New Brick on Hanover Street in 1721 and Christ Church on Salem Street in 1723 (known today as the "Old North Church"). The

North End also had a substantial working class, as the mechanics employed a number of journeymen and laborers in their shops and yards, while the upper class required many servants and slaves. When Bonner created his map, the population of Boston was approximately twelve thousand, with about two thousand African Americans, or 17 percent. As Boston's most populous and desirable neighborhood, the North End would have been the most sought-after zip code in the country, had there been such codes at the time. Boston was and continued to be the largest town in British North America until about 1750, when it was overtaken by Philadelphia and New York City.

Sights and Sounds

In the mid-eighteenth century, the North End was filled with the commotion of business and everyday life, just as it is today. As a seaport and a neighborhood dominated by shipyards and surrounded by wharves and sailing vessels, the most common sights and sounds (and smells) were associated with the ocean. Fishermen would bring in their ships filled with cod, mackerel or mollusks like oysters and clams to unload their catches. Although Faneuil Hall was built in 1742 as a central market for Boston, many businesspeople resisted a set schedule and location for selling their goods. Once fresh fish were examined by an appointed "Culler of Fish" (inspector), peddlers could buy quantities from the fishermen or from middlemen. Throughout the day, peddlers would push their carts through the streets of the North End and yell out what they had for sale. Their voices would mingle with the sounds of hammering and sawing from the shipyards, the rattling of horses and carts along the cobblestone streets and the conversation of thousands of North Enders.

Wooden structures with gardens coexisted with brick dwellings and green space throughout the district, and very few of these homes had more than three floors. Every home had at least one chimney, and the smoke and aromas escaping them were another ever-present part of life in the North End. Soot and other dirt could collect in chimneys, which were prone to burning, a process that town records called "flaming out." Flames from a dirty chimney could set the roof on fire, which had the natural ability to spread to neighboring buildings. African Americans, either free people or those enslaved people allowed spare time to work for their own money, were often hired to clean the chimneys. In fact, the first African-American employee in Boston, appointed in 1689, was a chimney sweeper. Jeremiah, whose surname was not recorded, continued in that important fire prevention position for five years. Low, long warehouses and sheds, and some small dwellings, could be

Ebenezer Clough built this house on Unity Street in 1712. It is one of the few surviving examples of early eighteenth-century middle-class architecture in downtown Boston. The building is owned by the Old North Foundation.

found on the docks along the waterfront, along with lime kilns, soap boiling shops and other fragrant industries. Mills, breweries and refineries were set up around the Mill Pond, adding to the olfactory experience. Unfortunately, local custom was to throw the bodies of dead dogs, cats and other pets into the Mill Pond, along with a variety of garbage, which together contributed to the already numerous hazards to public health.

The waterfront area along North Street and near North Square also had many taverns, beginning as early as 1652. Colonial taverns were the only places where a visitor could eat and drink if he didn't know anyone in town. North Enders could also refresh themselves at these establishments, which became the main gathering places for local men; here, they exchanged the latest world news, discussed Boston politics and traded in the freshest local gossip. The selectmen increasingly approved "cook's shops" and "vicktualing houses" as the town grew in the mid-1600s, and various individuals were licensed to "draw beere" or sell "strong watters." Entrepreneurs could conduct this sort of business from their homes and did not have to keep a regular inn or tavern like the Red Lion or the Salutation.

The style and age of this early eighteenth-century house at 350–352 Hanover Street, at the corner of Tileston Street, is similar to the nearby Clough House, but it is easy to miss when walking along Hanover Street. Some historians believe that this was the birthplace of Paul Revere, though that has not yet been substantiated.

Church steeples dominated the skyline, especially on Hanover Street. Prior to 1714, there were only two houses of worship in the North End: the North Meeting House on North Square and First Baptist on the edge of the Mill Pond, near what is today the intersection of Stillman and North Margin Streets. Both meetinghouses were made of wood, and First Baptist did not have a steeple at that time. In the decade after 1714, three new religious structures were added to the neighborhood: New North, New Brick and Christ Church. New Brick, a congregational meetinghouse like New North, was completed in 1721, and its steeple was surmounted by a brass weather vane in the shape of a cockerel (young rooster). The sanctuary and tower of Christ Church, an Anglican church, were completed on Salem Street in 1723, but the tall steeple was not built and attached to the building until 1740. A local man named Shem Drowne, who was a deacon of the First

Baptist Church, made the weather vane for Christ Church, in the shape of a flowing banner, and the cockerel on New Brick, as well as the famous grasshopper still atop Faneuil Hall. On Sunday, the day of rest, reflection and prayer, the bells of the churches called the townspeople to worship, at which point the North End became relatively quiet.

The Streets

During Boston's first half century, twenty-three streets were created in the North End. Some were ordered by the selectmen, while others grew out of common usage. In 1636, the town's leaders declared that "Inhabitants of the towne Shall have libertie to appoint men for the setting of [streets], as need shall require." This provided the legal basis necessary for landowners to create paths and passageways through or around their property so long as they did not obstruct other streets. The largest roads, such as North, Hanover, Charter and Prince, were built prior to 1650, along with ten shorter streets and lanes. In the next two decades, nine additional streets, all small lanes except for Salem Street, were built through government-approved private efforts. Thus, a basic street pattern emerged by 1679 and has survived to the present day. No buildings of any kind have survived from that year, nor have the ferries, mills, the battery or the North Meeting House. Even the tombstones in the cemetery on Copp's Hill have been stolen, vandalized and rearranged over time. The streets of the North End remain the largest and most tangible connection to local history.

In the 1600s, permanent streets were demarcated with stakes or poles at various intervals and were eventually paved with smooth stones. A gutter or "conduit" ran through the center of larger streets for rainwater and small debris. Regularly lighted streets would not be maintained until the 1770s, and sidewalks made of wooden boards were not instituted until the early 1800s. Shorter lanes and alleys, which usually occupied the spaces between estates and were often only four or five feet wide, were not paved nor necessarily marked. Despite laws to the contrary, Boston's streets were constantly littered with horse manure, scraps of cloth or leather from the tailor shops, rotting entrails from the butcher shops and, like the Mill Pond, dead animals. It was the tedious and thankless job of the "Surveyors of the Highways" and "Water Bailiffs" to patrol the streets and the waterfront for garbage and attempt to enforce the cleanliness laws, while simultaneously stopping individuals for galloping their horses in the busy streets or young children for kicking balls and roughhousing.

The First Street Name in Boston

As Boston entered the eighteenth century, its streets remained officially nameless. During the seventeenth century, there had simply been no need. The population of the entire town is estimated at three thousand for the year 1660, and though it rose steadily from the beginning, it was only about seven thousand at the close of the century. With so few people, and relatively few landmarks, there was no practical reason to affix names. For example, medium-sized universities in New England today have between nine thousand and sixteen thousand undergraduate students living on their campuses. There are various paths throughout each campus that, even if they were assigned official names by the school administration, would be known to the students and easily recognized by a variety of colloquial monikers. So it was with Bostonians who used different descriptions of and references to the nameless streets in almost every instance.

Between 1699 and 1702, the selectmen enlarged the cemetery on Copp's Hill, opened a writing school in the North End, formalized bylaws for the entire town and initiated the building of a firehouse for the water engine. The expanding population, as well as the increase in visitors from around the world, necessitated the growth of government and public services, which in turn created a historical moment of opportunity to name the streets. Samuel and Hannah Sewall provided the catalyst for the project when they established a memorial to Hannah's parents on May 21, 1701. Hannah's father was John Hull, the first mint master of Massachusetts. His fortunes grew from this position, as well as his inter-colonial investments and trading agreements. John and his wife, Judith, had only one child, Hannah, who married Samuel Sewall in 1676.

Hannah inherited two-thirds of her father's estate upon his death in 1683, making Sewall a very wealthy man. Hannah presumably inherited what was left of her mother's holdings when Judith Hull passed away in 1695. In addition to the house they all shared in the South End, Samuel and Hannah also came into possession of property adjacent to Copp's Hill Burying Ground in the North End. They deeded part of the land to the Town of Boston "for the conveniency & accommodation of the Inhabitants," with the stipulation that a strip of land "laid out for a high-way or Street running through our field…be for ever hereafter called & known by the name of Hull Street." In 1701, Hull Street was situated between Salem and Snowhill Streets, to the south of the cemetery, and was not extended down to Commercial Street until 1828. The words "Hull Street" were written largely in the text of the Sewalls' deed. The name was not only a lasting tribute to Hannah's parents, but it was also the first official, permanent name of a street in Boston. It was not explicitly stated in the deed that this was a memorial to John and Judith. Bostonians did not record why they chose particular street names, assuming, perhaps, that the reason for each name would be obvious to anyone living at the time, as was the case with Hull Street.

Because the selectmen had agreed to preserve the name of one street, they voted on September 22, 1701, to name all of the rest. The vote passed without any recorded discussion, stating that "the Select men of this Town are impowered to Assign and affix Names unto the Severall streets & Lanes within this Town, so as they shall judg meet and convenient." This project, unprecedented in Boston, was not completed for nearly seven years, and during those intervening years it was not discussed again in the town records. At their meeting on May 8, 1708, the selectmen listed and adopted names for Boston's 110 streets, lanes, alleys, squares, courts and ways without explanation. Many changes have occurred since 1708, and only fourteen streets in the North End have retained their original names. Bartholomew Green, a Boston bookseller, printed the first list on a broadside with three columns, and the reasoning for some of the names has confounded historians for the last three centuries. This is in part why the narrow and winding alleys of the North End are of special interest to hundreds of thousands of visitors each year. The temptation to walk on streets that people have been using for nearly four hundred years, along with the real possibility of finding a historical treasure around any corner, is irresistible.

Pope's Day

North Enders rolled a giant effigy of the pope surrounded by lights and music through the streets every November. The Pope's Day festivities grew larger and more intense at the time of Boston's centennial, due in large part to the increased number of people available to participate. When the celebrations began, the North End was the most populous part of Boston, and for a time only North Enders created the annual float and paraded it throughout the town. Boston's Pope's Day originated in England when, on November 5, 1605, a man named Guy Fawkes was arrested for planting barrels of gunpowder underneath the English House of Lords. Fawkes was Catholic, and he and nearly a dozen others conspired to blow up the House of Lords in order to kill the king and most of the members of Parliament, ushering in England's return to a Catholic state. After his arrest, Fawkes was interrogated, tortured and killed. Although the "Gunpowder Plot" was certainly not forgotten in England, it did not become a major day of remembrance until the end of the seventeenth century. By the early 1700s, perhaps beginning with the centennial of the treasonous event, "Guy Fawkes Day" was celebrated with bonfires, including burning an effigy of Fawkes; later, fireworks were added to the celebration. Today, fireworks are still used to commemorate November 5 in the United Kingdom.

These celebrations made their way to the English settlements across North America. In Boston, as in other towns, a large float was created to hold the effigies. The float consisted of two platforms, sometimes as long as forty feet and often as wide as ten feet. Large wheels were connected to the lower platform, and the upper platform was situated about five feet above the lower. This would give people enough space to stand between the platforms in order to operate the movements of the effigies. Because Guy Fawkes was part of a Catholic conspiracy, the Roman Catholic Church and its leader, the pope, were especially maligned on November 5, in a celebration that came to be called Pope's Day, or sometimes Pope Night. Fawkes himself, however, seems to have been forgotten, and the North End float usually carried life-sized effigies of the pope, the devil and other suspected Catholic or political enemies. The effigies were translucent, and lanterns were placed inside them to make them glow as they made their way through the streets of Boston. There were no regular streetlights in the town before 1773, so the gruesome images must have been particularly striking after nightfall. Revelers sang, drummed and fiddled on the float, sounds that could easily be heard across the small town in the crisp autumn air. Any Catholics who were unfortunate enough to be in Boston on November 5 must have feared for their safety as the procession grew louder and the participants became drunk and rowdy.

It was not long before the South End began building a float of its own. After traversing that part of the town, the South End float would meet the North End float, which had just finished traveling its own streets, and they would pass relatively peacefully so that they could parade in the opposite neighborhood. Each float would stop in front of the homes of the more prosperous residents and ask for money to pay for the evening's festivities. Fearing damage to their property should they refuse, most of Boston's well-to-do made their contributions. At the end of the night, North Enders would burn their float on Copp's Hill in a great bonfire, followed by a feast and more drinking, while the South End float and celebration took place on Boston Common. By the 1740s, however, a rivalry between the two neighborhoods created a different ending to the night. After the neighborhoods completed their parades, each group tried to capture the other's float, especially the pope effigy. The winning group would get to burn its captured pope in its own neighborhood. The rivalry quickly turned violent, and each year the North End and South End gangs beat each other without restraint. Later, as tensions grew between Great Britain and its American colonies, Revolutionary leaders in Boston co-opted the usual Pope's Day activities for their own political purposes.

CHAPTER 5

NEIGHBORHOOD OF REVOLUTION

The Boston census taken at the end of 1742 revealed a population of 16,382, the highest point it would reach until the close of the century. Among the citizens of Boston was the future Revolutionary War leader Samuel Adams, who would complete his master's degree at Harvard the following year. He chose as his thesis topic "Whether it be lawful to resist the Supreme Magistrate if the Commonwealth cannot otherwise be preserved." At twenty-one years of age, Adams had absorbed the lessons of the Enlightenment, and he would later argue that government must draw its power from the people, who naturally have inalienable rights. In other words, the rights of Americans are not provisionally granted by a monarch, and they cannot be voted away by a majority of citizens. These were groundbreaking ideas in the early eighteenth century, and there was not yet a nation in the world based on them. Thomas Hutchinson, who was thirty-two when Samuel Adams was studying at Harvard, never really understood Adams's position. Throughout his years in public service, Hutchinson always defended the rights of Massachusetts but never stopped believing that those rights were derived from the authority of the king and Parliament. He worried that if the colonies became independent from Great Britain, some other nation would overpower them, and Americans under any other nation would certainly have fewer rights. Hutchinson thought that the best an American could do was live a comfortable life as the subject of a distant British king. He did not anticipate that soon Americans would rather die free than live as "subjects."

Thomas Hutchinson was born in the North End, and as a leader of the royal government of Massachusetts, he was a central figure in the years leading up to the Revolution. Hutchinson was educated in the Tileston Street school buildings provided to the neighborhood by his wealthy family.

Thomas Hutchinson (1711–1780) of Garden Court Street, 1741. *Courtesy of the Massachusetts Historical Society.*

He went on to Harvard and then spent several successful years in business. He entered public service in Massachusetts with his election to the legislature in 1737. During his first two decades as a lawmaker, he helped stabilize Massachusetts's currency, fought against impressment of Massachusetts men by the British navy and drafted the "Albany Plan of Union" with Benjamin Franklin. The plan, written during the early days of the French and Indian

War, called for a continental assembly and united action on the part of the English colonies. Unfortunately, the various colonies still had not learned to work together, and the plan was not implemented. During his first quarter century in public service, Hutchinson was regarded as a smart legislator. No one could have imagined that in 1765 he would be stoned or that his house would be destroyed by angry Bostonians.

Attack in North Square

As the Pope's Day rivalry became more intense between the North and South Ends at mid-century, the gangs became more organized. Each neighborhood had its own captain and lieutenants to organize the event, build the floats and orchestrate activities throughout the night. Local tradition says that the North End usually beat the South End, but it is not possible to know all the details of those intoxicated outdoor spectacles. It is known that government officials could do nothing to stop the violence, even after a boy was killed during the Pope's Day fighting in 1764. That year, the South End defeated its rival under the leadership of its captain, Ebenezer McIntosh. During the following winter, the British Parliament passed the Stamp Act, requiring British subjects in America to pay for a special stamp on all of their legal documents, commercial contracts, pamphlets, newspapers and other printed items. Businessmen, politicians and especially lawyers would be directly impacted by the new law, and people from that group, like Samuel Adams and James Otis, orchestrated public opposition to the act. Adams was able to consolidate the North End and South End gangs under the leadership of McIntosh, and he convinced McIntosh to lead the populace in demonstrations against the Stamp Act rather than pointless, anti-Catholic brawls.

Samuel Adams, and others like him in the Whig political party, believed that Parliament had no right to directly tax the American colonies because there were no elected American representatives in Parliament. On August 14, 1765, McIntosh led the united gang to the Liberty Tree in the South End, where they hung an effigy of Andrew Oliver. After many Pope's Days, McIntosh and his men were skilled at building effigies. Oliver had been appointed to distribute the stamps in Massachusetts, and he hoped to profit from the appointment. As the enforcer of the Stamp Act, however, he became the target for the Whigs' demonstrations. Oliver's brother-in-law, Thomas Hutchinson, was the lieutenant governor at the time and ordered the sheriff to remove the effigy. Upon seeing the size of the crowd gathered at the Liberty Tree, the frightened sheriff did not dare to remove the likeness of Oliver. As the Governor's Council met at the Old State House to determine how to best handle the problem, McIntosh and his men cut the effigy down themselves so that they could parade it through the town. The gang marched the effigy loudly past the Old State House on its way to a small building that Oliver had just built in the vicinity. Oliver had ordered the building to be constructed for use as shops, and the mob believed that he was storing the stamps there. It did not take them long to completely pull the building apart.

After leaving the site of Oliver's shop building, the crowd marched to Oliver's house, located nearby, where those in the home could clearly see crowd members behead the effigy. The frightening decapitation was followed by a storm of rocks and other debris, which did considerable damage to Oliver's house. From there, the gang marched on to the summit of Fort Hill and built a bonfire out of the wood from Oliver's dismantled shop and burned what was left of his "body." After this gruesome spectacle, McIntosh led his men back to Oliver's house, where they began to systematically destroy it in search of Oliver himself. The would-be stamp agent had already vacated the house and, upon the advice of friends, sought refuge with the king's troops at a Boston Harbor fort called Castle William (known today as the site of Fort Independence). Even though the governor and the commander of the local militia had decided earlier that there was nothing they could do to stop the mob, Lieutenant Governor Hutchinson was appalled by this direct attack on a royal official (as well as a family member).

Hutchinson took the sheriff with him to confront McIntosh and the others as they destroyed Oliver's house. This unfortunate decision resulted in the two men running from the scene under a barrage of rocks and other debris. Oliver resigned as the stamp agent the next day, but McIntosh found a new target in Hutchinson, who had identified himself as a supporter of the Stamp Act by supporting Oliver. On the night of August 26, while out drinking and destroying property, McIntosh's men marched into the North End and up to Hutchinson's mansion on Garden Court Street at the edge of North Square. They looted and nearly destroyed the house and uprooted and mangled the beautiful garden. Hutchinson and his family were lucky to escape with their lives. Only the sobering light of the following morning stopped the fury of the mob, which was still pulling the house apart. This violence was more than Whig political leaders had intended, and it was making them look less than principled to lawmakers in London. The fury of the attack by a largely working-class group also struck fear in the wealthy residents of the town, who might otherwise have supported bonfires, marches and other rambunctious, but largely nondestructive, political protest.

The Hutchinson House on Garden Court Street. *Courtesy of the Boston Public Library, Print Department.*

It was for this reason that Whig leaders convinced McIntosh to change his plans for the fifth of November. Rather than building their floats and ending the night with a violent brawl, the men of the North End and the South End marched in peaceful protest of the Stamp Act through the streets on November 5, 1765. They sat down that night to an enormous feast paid for by wealthy Bostonians who opposed the Stamp Act, particularly John Hancock. Pope's Day celebrations would reemerge over the next decade, but never again did the two neighborhoods of Boston fight for supremacy. A poster printed a few years after the attack on Hutchinson's home has survived. It was created by the young men who participated in the old Pope's Days, and it commemorated and encouraged the continued revelries of November 5 but also recognized how the neighborhoods had united. In the upper left corner of the poster, the words "South End Forever" appear, and in the upper right it reads, "North End Forever." Every strata of Boston society, with the exception of the ruling Tory party, had come together on Pope's Day in 1765 for a peaceful political protest of London's policies. This type of activism was respectable enough to keep old friends and win new ones in Parliament, and it proved to Adams, McIntosh and other "Sons of Liberty," as they were thereafter known, that a properly controlled mob could ignore the law and rule the town of Boston.

Sugar, Stamps and Hancock's Wine

At the close of the French and Indian War in 1763, France lost Canada to the kingdom of Great Britain, and the British government instituted a series of taxes on the American colonies to help pay for the long and expensive conflict, in addition to future defense costs. The British prime minister, George Grenville, decided to reinvigorate a tax that had been on the books for thirty years—a tax on imported sugar and molasses. Both items were major trade commodities between New England and the West Indies, and molasses in particular was used to make rum, another key revenue producer. Back in 1733, when the original tax had been passed, Boston alone was distilling approximately 1.3 million gallons of rum from West Indian molasses every year. British officials were quite aware that American merchants, especially those in New England, had been avoiding for years the six-pence-per-gallon tax on these popular products through bribery and smuggling. In 1764, Grenville actually lowered the amount of the tax but extended it beyond sugar and molasses to include coffee, different types of wine and certain textiles. He also ordered customs officials to strictly enforce the tax, as well as the new, more cumbersome regulations on the export of lumber, another high-volume New England commodity, to any country but Great Britain. As a result, the economy in Boston, which generally counted on lenient law enforcement, was severely disrupted.

Bostonians protested the Sugar Act chiefly through boycotts of goods made in England, hoping to simultaneously avoid taxes and hinder the economy across the Atlantic. The protests became violent with the implementation of the subsequent Stamp Act. Despite the boycotts and the destruction of property, Parliament passed more taxes on the colonies. One of the wealthiest men in Boston, John Hancock tried to keep his businesses afloat and his profit margins high. Hancock owned a large wharf below Fleet Street in the North End, about where Lewis Wharf is today. In the early summer of 1768, one of his small ships, the *Liberty*, arrived at his wharf with a cargo of Madeira wine. Customs officials attempted to seize the *Liberty* because Hancock had not paid taxes on the wine. The Sons of Liberty marched through the North End and down to the wharf, where they forced the customs officers to run

The Church in Brattle Square attracted some of the most influential members of Boston society, including John Hancock, Samuel Adams and Harrison Gray Otis. Two of this church's ministers were memorialized with street names in the North End. They were Samuel Cooper (1725–1783), part of the inner circle of Boston Revolutionaries, and Peter Thacher (1752–1802), a founder of the Massachusetts Historical Society. *Private collection.*

for their lives. The Sons portrayed Hancock as another victim of oppression, though it was quite clear that he was caught smuggling, and mob violence was becoming even more commonplace in the Massachusetts capital.

Massachusetts governor Francis Bernard asked London for troops to maintain order in Boston, and a British fleet arrived in Boston Harbor at the end of September. Hundreds of soldiers disembarked at Long Wharf and

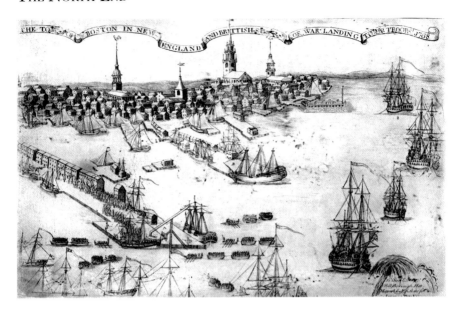

A View of Part of the Town of Boston in New England and Brittish Ships of War Landing Their Troops, 1768. This is a portion of a facsimile engraving of Paul Revere's 1770 print. The North Battery can be seen at the far right. Revere exaggerated the size of the churches, which are, from right to left, New North, Christ Church, Old North Meeting House and New Brick (with its conspicuous rooster). *Courtesy of the Boston Public Library, Print Department.*

marched into the town, beating their drums and flying their colors. Even though they were subjects of the same government as the soldiers, Bostonians felt as though they were being invaded by a conquering army. North Enders, like all Bostonians, now encountered uniformed and armed soldiers in their streets and off-duty soldiers looking for part-time work, which meant fewer jobs for locals. In addition to the presence of the troops, British ships of war remained anchored in the harbor, ready to subdue the town if necessary. Paul Revere made an engraving of the arrival of the troops, and he used it to help his fellow Sons of Liberty spread the word about the government's continued attempts to rob them of their rights.

Bloodshed on Hanover Street

The Sons of Liberty coordinated their boycott of British goods with local merchants, though some merchants still bought and sold English imports. These "Loyalist" stores were often surrounded by protesters and occasionally had their windows broken or suffered garbage or even excrement on their façades. Ebenezer Richardson, an employee of the Customs Office, attempted to collect the necessary taxes from Loyalist merchants and informed the Customs Office when people smuggled and sold British goods, thereby becoming a very unpopular man with the majority of local residents. On February 22, 1770, Richardson came to the aid of a Loyalist merchant whose shop had been targeted by boycotters. The crowd became angry at Richardson, and he exchanged unpleasantries with them even after he had left the shop and walked back down Hanover Street to his home, not far from the corner of Richmond Street.

Once at home, Richardson continued to argue with the crowd, which was steadily growing. It wasn't long before some of the young boys began throwing trash and rocks at the house. Richardson went inside and soon returned to the doorway with a gun "presented upon the people indiscriminately," according to the *Boston Evening Post*. Rather than scaring the harassers away, they grew louder, continued to throw stones and started breaking windows. Richardson retreated into the house, but after a few minutes he aimed his gun at Hanover Street and fired into the crowd. A young man named Samuel Gore was shot in his leg and his right hand, though he survived his injuries, continued to be an active Patriot and thrived as a painter and entrepreneur after the war. An eleven-year-old boy named Christopher Seider was also shot. He was wounded in the arm and chest, and his lungs were punctured. Despite their earlier angry behavior, the crowd was stunned to see the wounded young people lying in the street, and a few bystanders ran into the nearby New Brick Meeting House and rang the bell. New Brick's large bell, like the others in town, was used not only to call people to meeting but also to announce celebrations, mourn disasters and warn of fire. When North Enders heard the bell tolling on that shocking February day, they responded by running to Hanover Street near New Brick. They found the wounded Gore, the dying Seider and a crowd angry at Richardson, who was still ensconced in his house.

Enough men had arrived to surround Richardson's house and force their way in via a rear door. They overwhelmed Richardson, pried the weapon from his hands and carried him off to Faneuil Hall. Four magistrates were summoned to the hall, where Richardson was deposed "before at least a thousand people," according to the *Boston News-Letter*. The magistrates ordered Richardson to be committed to the jail to await trial. En route from Faneuil Hall, the crowd was so angry at Richardson that "had not Gentleman of influence interposed, [he] never would have reached the prison." Later that evening, Seider died of his wounds. The Sons of Liberty seized on the terrible incident and proclaimed that the boy was a martyr.

Samuel Adams arranged an elaborate funeral for Seider, who was the son of German immigrants, and over two thousand people attended the procession and burial. Seider was laid to rest at the Granary Burying Ground in a coffin inscribed with Latin phrases, which, when translated, mean "the serpent is lurking in the grass" and "innocence itself is nowhere safe." The Boston Sons of Liberty always portrayed themselves as innocent, and it was Parliament's actions and agents who were the lurking serpents.

The Sons continued to argue that as long as soldiers occupied Boston in a time of peace, tragedies like this were inevitable. Tensions continued to mount in the town, and less than two weeks later, on March 5, an enormous crowd surrounded and harassed British soldiers stationed near the Massachusetts capitol, known today as the Old State House. The besieged soldiers eventually fired into the crowd, instantly and mortally wounding five men. The Boston Massacre was captured in an engraving by Paul Revere, which showed the soldiers attacking a peaceful group of citizens. The engraving was circulated throughout the colonies, and it helped to build antagonism toward the British government. In addition, Samuel Adams coordinated an enormous funeral procession for the victims, who were buried next to Christopher Seider. To prevent further incidents, the troops were removed from the town and housed at Castle William. After these disturbing events, Parliament repealed most of the remaining colonial taxes, except for the tax on tea, and Boston was relatively devoid of similar violence for a couple of years.

The North End Caucus

Samuel Adams was a member of the Massachusetts legislature from 1765 through 1774, and he used his position there in the early 1770s to not only strengthen the opposition movement but also to communicate effectively with the legislative bodies of other colonies. Adams was a member of a group that called itself the North End Caucus, which helped to guarantee his continued reelection. The purpose of the caucus was to meet and decide whom the voters would put forth as candidates for the various elective public offices. Once the North End Caucus made a decision, it would send representatives to meet with the South End Caucus and the smaller caucus in the middle part of the town, which included the growing West End. The North End Caucus met alternately at the Salutation Tavern on Salutation Street, close to North Street, and at the Green Dragon Tavern, which was in the vicinity of Hanover and Blackstone Streets, not far from the bar of the same name located on Marshall Street today. John Adams, Paul Revere and

Joseph Warren were also members of the North End Caucus in the early 1770s, and the subject of imported tea was a major topic of discussion at their meeting on November 2, 1773.

In the spring of 1773, Parliament had offered an effective monopoly on tea sales in the American colonies to the nearly bankrupt East India Company. The bailout exempted the East India Company from the tea taxes, allowing it to undersell American merchants. In addition, Parliament assigned a small handful of merchants in each port to sell the East India tea. In Boston, two of Thomas Hutchinson's sons, Elisha and Thomas, were designated as legal tea retailers. At their November meeting, the North End Caucus knew that ships carrying the hated tea would arrive in Boston soon. The caucus decided that the Hutchinsons, and the other tea merchants, had accepted positions that were "destructive to this Community," and they were now "enemies to their Country." The men of the North End Caucus decided at that same meeting that "this body are determined that the Tea shipped or to be shipped by the East India Company shall not be landed." Thus, the North End's most active political organization formed the resolution that eventually resulted in the destruction of over three hundred crates of tea. The event is remembered today as the Boston Tea Party.

The End of Thomas Hutchinson

Lieutenant Governor Thomas Hutchinson became acting governor in 1769, and he officially assumed the position of governor in 1771. He was a constant target of Whig politicians, his effigy was burned with the others on Pope's Day and he was excoriated in the press when his relatives were appointed stamp agents and tea merchants. Governor Hutchinson regularly wrote letters to friends and colleagues in England to share proposals and urge action to bring political stability back to Massachusetts. No matter what his personal opinions were about certain policies (he had privately disapproved of the Stamp Act, for example), Hutchinson always publicly supported Parliament. In one of his letters he suggested that colonial liberty might have to be curtailed in order to restore order. This private letter, and others, was stolen in England and later offered to Benjamin Franklin, who was in London lobbying on behalf of the American colonies. Franklin sent all of the letters back to Boston, where they were leaked in the press during the summer of 1773. The press made Hutchinson out to be the personification of a greedy Loyalist official who wanted nothing more than to trample on the rights and liberties of common Americans. In truth, Hutchinson was an honest man from the North End with over thirty-five years of faithful public service to Massachusetts, but he was unwilling or incapable of seeing the point of view of those we now call Patriots. Hutchinson was probably the most hated man in America when he was recalled to London shortly after the Boston Tea Party. Although he always longed and expected to return to his native Massachusetts, Hutchinson died in exile in 1780.

CHAPTER 6

PAUL REVERE

Across the United States Paul Revere is celebrated as a Patriot, and it is safe to say that he is still the most famous North Ender. Revere's father was a French immigrant named Apollos Rivoire, who arrived in Boston at the age of thirteen to complete his apprenticeship as a goldsmith. Rivoire changed his name to Paul Revere, and he married Deborah Hitchborn, whose ancestors had been in America for generations. The exact birthplace of their eldest surviving son, the Patriot Paul Revere, is not known, but it was probably near where his father set up shop as a goldsmith in 1730. The shop was most likely on Hanover Street, near Tileston Street, when Paul was born in December 1734. Revere was baptized at the New Brick Meeting House, where his parents worshiped, and was educated at the North Writing School on Tileston Street. The Revere family had moved down by the waterfront to at least two different locations by the time Revere was eight years old. They finally settled near the head of Clark's Wharf, close to the corner of North and Fleet Streets, and that was where Revere spent the rest of his youth. Young Paul was apprenticed to his father and learned the goldsmith's trade. He was nineteen when his father died, and it fell to him and his widowed mother to continue his father's business. Except for interruptions caused by the French and Indian War and the War of Independence, Revere flourished and expanded his business as a silversmith and goldsmith for the rest of the century.

Paul Revere was well known throughout the town of Boston, not only as a talented artist and businessman, but also as one of the most active leaders of the Revolutionary movement. He was a Mason, a Son of Liberty and a member of both the North End Caucus and the Long Room Club, which was a more elite political group. In an America that was much more stratified than it is today, Revere was able to spend time among, and be liked

Paul Revere (1734–1818) of North Square, 1768. *Photograph ©2009 Museum of Fine Arts, Boston.*

by, Harvard-educated doctors and lawyers, the journeymen and apprentices in the shipyards or in his own shop and his fellow mechanics. This made him an important facilitator of communication between the various parts of Boston society and allowed him to constantly gather information that could prove useful to the movement. In addition, many of his colleagues were also customers, and he made new political connections with some of the people who patronized his shop. During the late 1760s, Boston's economy slowed, and Revere used his abilities as a silversmith to create political engravings, which were then copied and widely distributed. His 1770 engraving of the Boston Massacre is probably the single most famous image connected with that bloody affair.

Ghosts in North Square

Paul Revere and his wife and children moved to his now famous house, which still stands on North Square, in 1770. According to the *Boston Gazette*, Revere mounted "a very striking Exhibition" on the "never-to-be-forgotten Fifth of March" in 1771. On that first anniversary of the massacre, Revere built three illuminated displays, and in the evening he placed them in three different windows upstairs in his house. Revere's probable participation in past Pope's Day festivities meant that he had experience building large effigies lit by internal lanterns. In the first window was the ghost of Christopher Seider, who was attempting to stop the flow of blood from his wounds, while his friends stood near him weeping. Near the ghost was an obelisk, the names of the men killed in the massacre and the words, "Seider's pale Ghost fresh-bleeding stands, And Vengeance for his Death demands." In the next window was a bloody re-creation of the massacre, over which was written "FOUL PLAY." In the last display was the figure of a woman, who represented America, surrounded by symbols of liberty and resistance, with one foot on the head of a royal soldier and one finger pointing at the massacre. It was a gruesome and powerful display that brought "many Thousands" of spectators to North Square, which otherwise had no lighting. As the crowd stared at Paul Revere's House, onlookers were "struck with a solemn Silence," and their faces "were covered with a melancholy Gloom." At nine o'clock, the bells of the meetinghouses began tolling in remembrance, augmenting Revere's exhibition for its last hour. The artistry and pageantry of that night, combined with other events during the day, helped to keep the Revolutionary fervor alive during the years between the Massacre and the Tea Party.

Paul Revere's Rides

On December 17, 1773, Paul Revere made the first of more than a dozen rides on horseback to share news, gather intelligence or sound alarms. On this occasion he rode to New York and Philadelphia to explain the reasoning behind the Tea Party of the previous day, in which he most likely

Paul Revere's House, circa 1900. This image was taken before the 1907–1908 restoration. The Banca Italiana (literally "Italian Bank") and Filippo A. Goduti's cigar factory were housed there, as was what appears to be an Italian postal service. *Courtesy of the Museum of African American History, Boston, Massachusetts.*

participated, and to solicit the responses of Patriots in those towns. Five months later, Revere made a similar ride to tell about the consequences of the Boston Port Act, which ordered the closure of the Port of Boston for the outrageous destruction of the East India tea. Parliament suspended the civilian government, and General Thomas Gage, commander in chief of British forces in America, was subsequently appointed the military governor of Massachusetts. Gage's troops and warships enforced the closure of Boston Harbor, calculated to strangle the economy of the town until it submitted to the laws of the empire and paid for the tea.

Based in Boston, General Gage planned a series of short, surprise expeditions into the surrounding towns to disarm the colonists, who were drawing close to open rebellion. The largest supply of gunpowder was stored at the Powder House on the western side of Charlestown, now part of the city of Somerville. In the early morning hours of September 1, 1774, Gage's men successfully seized all of the powder and returned to Boston without causing alarm. Once the people of Massachusetts realized what had happened, a great panic spread throughout the towns, and many believed that a war had actually begun. After this "Powder Alarm" subsided, the panic turned to anger, and Paul Revere dispatched messengers to spread the news—the people of Massachusetts were ready now more than ever to resist British tyranny.

During 1774, the elected government of Massachusetts continued to meet in exile, and Whig leaders communicated with their colleagues in other colonies through Paul Revere, calling together a meeting of delegates representing all Americans. This Continental Congress met in September and October, and although Revere was not a delegate, he did bring to the congress the Suffolk Resolves, which called for resistance to the latest acts of Parliament, especially in light of the Powder House incident. British authorities had hoped that by punishing Massachusetts they would scare the other colonies into line. However, the other colonists were concerned that their laws and commerce could be arbitrarily disrupted. They came together in support of Massachusetts, rather than allowing the province to struggle and absorbing its international trade. Congress approved the Suffolk Resolves, and Paul Revere returned home with the news.

In the meantime, Gage planned other expeditions, and Revere received intelligence regarding the general's plans. Revere personally rode to Portsmouth, New Hampshire, in December to warn the populace that troops aimed to seize the ammunition at Fort William and Mary. Several hundred men from local militias gathered and assaulted the fort, which was guarded by a small garrison. The New Hampshire men overwhelmed the soldiers, took the fort and removed the gunpowder, which they brought to hiding places farther inland. Gage persisted after his failure in New Hampshire and sent a detachment of troops to Salem in February 1775. Though Revere was unable to learn the details of the plan, residents of Marblehead, where the troops landed after sailing from Boston, were organized. When the force arrived, they warned Salem, and the townspeople and militia were able to stop the march of the soldiers. As the day wore on, militia came from neighboring towns, and the soldiers were forced to return to Boston empty-handed.

By April 1775, Paul Revere was one of the last Whig leaders still in Boston, which was now under martial law. General Gage had fortified the entrance to Boston on the "neck" from Roxbury and had discontinued ferry service from the North End. In fact, a British warship, the *Somerset*, was anchored between the North End and Charlestown to prevent unauthorized crossings. The Sons of Liberty learned that Gage was about to receive new orders from London, approaching by ship, to arrest the rebellious leaders in Massachusetts and immediately end the growing conflict. On April 7, Revere rode to Concord to ensure that the town removed its significant store of munitions and hid them elsewhere. On April 16, knowing that the troops could march from Boston any day, Revere rode into the countryside again. This time, he traveled to Lexington to confer with the town leaders, as well as with Samuel Adams and John Hancock, who would certainly be targeted for detainment by Gage's new orders. On his way back, Revere stopped in Charlestown to discuss further plans and the reaction to a British expedition.

The Lanterns at the Old North Church

On April 18, British troops prepared to mobilize. After long weeks of idleness, the officers and soldiers were suddenly moving with energy and purpose, which of course raised suspicions in Boston. It was not long before General Gage's plan was discovered, and several people brought the news to Paul Revere. Revere met with Joseph Warren, and they agreed that Revere would attempt to escape from Boston via the North End in order to ride to Lexington and warn Hancock and Adams. It was not at all certain that he would be able to leave town, so William Dawes would also make the attempt to warn the two men who would represent Massachusetts at the Continental Congress the following month. Dawes planned to leave over the neck and through Roxbury. Unable to warn the people of Salem two months

The home of Robert Newman (1752–1804) on Salem Street, at the corner of Sheafe Street. *Courtesy of the Boston Public Library, Print Department.*

earlier, Revere had already worked out a backup plan with the Whig leaders in Charlestown. On the night of April 18, in case neither he nor Dawes could get out of Boston, Revere walked over to Salem Street to activate his emergency signal.

He walked to the Newman family home at the corner of Sheafe Street. The Newmans lived a block from Christ Church, which is known today as the Old North Church. Robert Newman's mother owned the house, and she was renting space to British officers. Newman, who was about twenty-three at the time, was the sexton, or caretaker, of Christ Church and had already agreed to assist Revere with the signal that night. To fool the officers, Newman had pretended to go to bed early. Instead, he snuck outside through a window and into the rear garden. Two other North Enders, John Pulling and Thomas Bernard, had agreed to help Revere with the signal as well. While the officers played cards in the front of the house,

Revere slipped around the back, where he found the three men waiting. He instructed them to hang two lanterns from the steeple of Christ Church, on the side facing Charlestown. This would warn the Sons of Liberty that Gage's men were about to leave Boston via the Charles River and march on Concord. Revere returned home to quickly prepare his escape from Boston. In the meantime, his three friends walked to the church, the tallest building in the area. Bernard stood guard while Pulling and Newman climbed into the steeple. Newman, who had the keys to the church, had prepared and hidden the lanterns inside the church earlier that day, and he and Pulling lit them, holding them out of the highest window of the steeple. Across the river in Charlestown, the local Whigs had been watching for Revere's signal, and when they saw the lanterns at about ten o'clock, they sprung into action. In addition to getting the word out, some men went to the edge of the river to watch for Revere's arrival.

The Most Famous Ride

Shortly after the lanterns were extinguished, Revere left his home on North Square and approached the Charles River, where two other friends were waiting to take him to Charlestown. Because Gage had shut down the ferry, Revere had to hide a small boat under a wharf, and because the *Somerset* guarded the mouth of the river, his friends had to muffle the oars. It is well known that Revere reached Charlestown, where he confirmed that his signal had been received earlier. He borrowed a horse and intended to ride to Lexington to warn Hancock and Adams to leave the area. After dodging British patrols on the road from Charlestown to Cambridge, Revere rode to Medford and then Arlington. In both towns, he sounded the alarm with local leaders, who in turn dispatched other riders to neighboring towns. Between Arlington and Lexington, farming communities with small populations, Revere stopped at almost every homestead to spread the word. He arrived at his destination at about midnight and successfully delivered his message. William Dawes arrived soon after, and, having completed their original mission, the two decided to continue on to Concord to convey the news themselves. Although they were both stopped by British patrols and never reached Concord, Revere had already personally alarmed four towns. In addition, he had set in motion other men who alarmed settlements as far away as Andover and Dracut before sunrise. By the time British troops reached Concord on the morning of April 19, hundreds of New England men stood ready. The British were defeated and pushed back into Boston, and the militia fortified positions in Roxbury and Charlestown to keep them surrounded.

The Siege of Boston

It is important to note that the ideals of the Revolution and the willingness of common people to fight for those ideals were not only to be found in Boston. In fact, the strength of the rebellion stemmed from the people across the many country towns and smaller seaports who believed in their natural, inalienable rights and the traditional self-governance of Massachusetts. It was these men and women who mobilized and kept the British military contained in Boston for two months after Lexington and Concord. Now that New England was in open rebellion, those who remained loyal to Great Britain took what they could and sought refuge in Boston under the protection of General Gage. At the same time, the population of Boston plummeted as people who supported the revolution left town, including Paul Revere and his family. Revere left his son, Paul, in Boston to look after his shop and home in North Square. The rest of the family moved to Watertown, which served as the capital of Massachusetts until Boston was liberated.

In an attempt to break out of Boston, General Gage fortified Copp's Hill and bombarded Charlestown on June 17, 1775, in what is known as the Battle of Bunker Hill. British ships surrounded the Charlestown peninsula, and British troops invaded the town to dislodge the Americans from their position on Breed's Hill. The British suffered very heavy losses, but they did win the battle and burned most of the town to the ground. Yet, the battle boosted American morale because of the heavy price they forced the British to pay and because of their relatively low number of casualties. General George Washington arrived in Watertown two weeks later and assumed command of the military forces at Cambridge on July 3.

As Washington prepared his army, Revere traveled to Pennsylvania to observe the only powder mill in the colonies so that he could help build one in Massachusetts. London would not allow any more powder to be imported in the colonies, but Revere was successful, and a mill was constructed in Canton. Throughout the rest of 1775, a stalemate ensued. In late January 1776, Colonel Henry Knox arrived from Fort Ticonderoga in New York with dozens of cannons and muskets, as well as thousands of rounds of ammunition. The weaponry had been captured along with the fort several months earlier, under the leadership of Ethan Allen. Once Knox returned to Boston, Washington ordered the cannons to be mounted at Dorchester

Heights and aimed at the British fleet in the harbor. With the town surrounded and the cannons aimed at their source of supplies and communication, the British position in Boston became untenable. On March 17, 1776, they, along with hundreds of Loyalists, were forced to evacuate the town, thus ending the Siege of Boston. March 17 is a legal holiday in Boston today: Evacuation Day.

The Destruction of Old North

Bostonians were now free to return to their town, and they found that many buildings had been pulled apart during the winter and used as firewood for heat and cooking. Many of the meetinghouses had been desecrated. For example, Old South had been used as a riding stable. British authorities had torn down the West Meeting House's steeple because they suspected that Americans were using it to signal to their fellow rebels in Cambridge. Only one meetinghouse was completely destroyed, however, and that was the original Old North Meeting House. The minister of Old North, John Lathrop, had spoken out from the pulpit against British authority. On January 16, 1776—just two months before General Washington drove the British soldiers from Boston—Old North was completely dismantled and used for firewood under orders from Gage's successor, General William Howe. It was never rebuilt. The congregation, under the leadership of Lathrop, merged with the New Brick, which had lost many of its members when the Loyalists left Boston. The combined congregations worshiped in the original 1721 building of New Brick and called themselves the Second Church in Boston. By contrast, the Old North Church, where the signal lanterns had been hung, was not harmed by British soldiers, though it did remain closed for several years.

During the Siege of Boston, one house of worship in the North End remained open: New North. Its minister, Andrew Eliot, continued to preach every Sabbath, and he welcomed the scattered citizens from any part of the town to join him. He avoided political discussions altogether, so as to continue his ministry during the occupation. After the siege ended, General Washington and his officers attended New North for a thanksgiving service by Reverend Eliot. He preached on Isaiah 33:20, which speaks of the holy city of Jerusalem that cannot be destroyed. The population in Boston, now numbering fewer than three thousand, was thankful that the military occupation was over.

CHAPTER 7

NEW REPUBLIC
ENTREPRENEURS

America's emancipation from Great Britain provided entrepreneurs
with opportunities to build domestic industries and create new trading
networks. North Enders like Paul Revere, Thomas Lewis, Samuel Shaw and
William Tudor invested in infrastructure, factories and trade, and utilized
a steady influx of newcomers to the Boston area as their new workforce.
Between 1790 and 1820, about one thousand people were added to the
number of residents in Boston each year. Due to the recent war, religion,
education, family and the compact size of their native neighborhood,
Revere and the other preexisting North End businessmen formed a closely
connected small group. Revere, Lewis, Shaw and Tudor had much in
common, yet an examination of their business activities after the Revolution
reveals their very different paths to commercial success in the early years of
the new nation.

Education for Business

The North End entrepreneurs shared a similar education. Revere, Shaw and
Tudor all attended the North Writing School, where they learned to read,
the basics of math and penmanship. These skills were essential not only for
further education and understanding scripture but also for success in business.
The original North Writing School was founded in 1700 under the direction
of Richard Henchman, the son of Daniel Henchman, who had himself
been a teacher some three decades earlier. Daniel Henchman owned land
along the waterfront, between Charter and Commercial Streets, and it is for
him that Henchman Street, originally laid out in the 1670s, was named. The
North Writing School did not have a permanent home until a new building

John Tileston (1736–1826) of Prince Street, 1818. *Courtesy of the Massachusetts Historical Society.*

was constructed at the end of 1718. Edward Hutchinson and his brother Thomas, the father of the future governor, paid for the building. The North Writing School was the most widely attended educational institution in the North End, and John Tileston was its master for almost sixty years.

John Tileston influenced generations of North End children, and Bostonians rewarded him for his work near the end of his life. Tileston was an assistant teacher at the North Writing School for a dozen years before becoming master in 1761. He did not teach Paul Revere because he was about two years younger, but Paul Revere Jr. was a student of Tileston's. Though Thomas Lewis did not grow up in Boston, Thomas Lewis Jr. was taught by Tileston, as were Samuel Shaw and his brothers, William Tudor and John Eliot, the son of Reverend Andrew Eliot. Tileston was beloved by his students, and he led his schoolboys in the parade welcoming President George Washington to Boston in 1789. Tileston remained in his teaching job until 1819. Because of his position at the school, he was connected to most North End families, both rich and poor.

Perhaps Tileston's most famous pupil was Edward Everett, who became a member of both houses of the United States Congress, as well as a governor of Massachusetts, president of Harvard and minister at the Brattle Street Church. Everett, who had a clear affection for his old teacher, recalled that Tileston constantly helped the needy in the community. In addition, Everett remembered that Tileston's desk was "a perfect curiosity shop of confiscated balls, tops, penknives, marbles, and jewsharps, the accumulation of forty years." Upon his retirement in 1819, the selectmen voted to continue paying Tileston's salary until his death, which came five years later. However, Tileston did live long enough to receive another honor from the town.

The John and Lydia Tileston House. The Tilestons lived here on Prince Street, at the corner of Margaret Street, at least in their old age. *Private collection.*

John Eliot (1754–1813) of Hanover Street, 1779. *Courtesy of the Massachusetts Historical Society.*

Tileston Street had been known as Love Street since 1708, named after the local property owners, John and Susanna Love. In 1821, Samuel Brown led a petition to rename Love Street in honor of the schoolmaster. Brown was a mast maker who lived near the school on Love Street and was most likely a former student of Tileston's. It may be reasonably asked why Samuel Brown and the others did not wish to name the school, rather than the street, after Tileston. The answer lies in the fact that John Tileston outlived his former student Reverend John Eliot. The school had been renamed for Eliot shortly after his death in 1813. John Tileston was so beloved and his tenure was so unusually long that on June 20, 1821, the selectmen voted to approve the petition and call the street Tileston Street from then on, even though the memorialized man was still alive.

Paul Revere

The popular story of Paul Revere ends with his ride to Lexington in 1775. However, he continued to lead a productive and patriotic life for more than thirty years after that famous night. After the evacuation, Revere and his family returned to Boston, and he joined the Massachusetts militia. Revere wanted a commission in the Continental army, but despite his many patriotic activities and wide network of friends, a commission never materialized. Instead, Lieutenant Colonel Revere was placed in command of Castle William and tasked with fortifying Boston, which feared a return of British troops. Revere also participated in two major expeditions. The first, to attack the British in Rhode Island, was aborted, and the second, to assault the British in Penobscot Bay, Maine, was a disaster. The top leaders of the Penobscot force made bad decisions and did not communicate well, and as a result several officers were disciplined or dismissed. Revere was forced to resign, but over the next three years he continually petitioned for a court-martial to investigate his conduct. State authorities finally granted his request, and his name was cleared in 1782.

By the early 1780s, Revere's son, Paul, was in charge of the day-to-day operations at his silver shop. Revere opened a hardware store near Faneuil Hall, where he sold a wide array of household items, jewelry, harnesses, buckles and the like made from metals such as silver and gold or alloys like brass and pewter. He advertised that he and his son produced objects "equal to any imported, and upon the lowest terms." Revere, out of patriotism and business savvy, encouraged Bostonians to buy locally made American products. In order to increase the range and amount of items he could produce for sale, Revere opened a foundry in 1788 on Foster Street in the North End, near the corner of Commercial Street. Now he could produce stoves, tools and bolts for nearby houses, shops and shipyards. He also made cannons and, within a few years, had taught himself how to cast bells. By 1792, the old bell at the Second Church was cracked and almost unusable. In the past, this situation would have required sending the bell abroad for repair or purchasing a new one from England. But in this case, Revere, who was a lifelong member of the Second Church, was able to recast and enlarge the bell right in the North End. It was the first bell ever cast in Boston, and it is still in existence today, though it is housed in St. James's Episcopal Church in Cambridge.

About three blocks down Commercial Street from Revere's foundry was Edmund Hartt's shipyard. As American merchant vessels spread across the globe, the federal government initiated a program to build up the U.S. Navy. Hartt was commissioned to build one of the new ships, and between 1794 and 1797, he constructed the USS *Constitution*. Revere supplied copper bolts and spikes and hundreds of other metal parts for the ship, and the *Constitution* spent its first decade at sea protecting U.S. ships in the Caribbean and the Mediterranean. Revere also made a range of weapons for the U.S. military and by 1800 was seeking to develop American capacity for rolling sheet copper to sheathe ships and protect the hulls. He built a copper rolling mill in Canton, Massachusetts, that year and rolled the copper for the refitting of the *Constitution*, which is still afloat today and is known as "Old Ironsides," in addition to many other government and private contracts. Revere also sold his house on North Square and moved to a larger house on Charter Street, near the corner of Hanover, closer to his Foster Street foundry. By 1804, Revere, at seventy years of age, moved his foundry operations to Canton and split his time between Canton and the North End. He was an active member of many civic and charitable organizations, as well as a very successful businessman, for the remainder of his life. Paul Revere died at his North End home in 1818. Not only had he played a key role in creating a new nation, but throughout his lifetime he also started a new industry (copper rolling) and supported the growth of the military and American trade.

Thomas Lewis

Whereas Paul Revere worked to increase American manufacturing capacity in the years after the Revolution, Thomas Lewis continued to conduct business as usual. Originally from Lynn, Lewis had a substantial wharf and trading business in Boston's North End by the 1780s. The North End's wharves housed warehouses and stores, where a wide range of agricultural products, as well as finished or processed items, could be purchased. Lewis's Wharf was an early version of a twentieth-century strip mall—a relatively self-contained row of stores constructed in an area where traffic lanes would allow the stores to receive large deliveries and capture the attention of as many shopping commuters as possible. Some of the items available on Lewis's Wharf were turpentine, tar, rice, cocoa, "Guadaloupe Cotton," "Jamaica fish," salt, white sugar, "Brown Havana sugars," gin and cod. Of course, Thomas Lewis did not stock and operate all of the stores on his wharf, and other merchants could rent stores of their own from him.

Judging by the items available, it is clear that Lewis was able to continue trading with the West Indies at a time when other Bostonians were focusing on the new trade with China. He also kept up the old North End tradition of selling products used in the shipyards, as well as buying and selling a variety of sloops, schooners and large ships. Lewis lived on North Street, not far from his wharf, and was a deacon of the Second Church. He sent his son Thomas to the North Writing School, and Thomas Jr. joined his father in the family business, which Lewis had renamed Thomas Lewis and Son by 1796. Thomas Lewis passed away in 1809, after a "long and very distressing" illness. His obituary in the *Boston Gazette* reported that he faced his illness with "patience and Christian fortitude" and that he was "a useful and industrious citizen, and…a good friend." Thomas Lewis Jr. continued to run the business until his own death in 1824. He was buried next to his father in Copp's Hill in the tomb that they had purchased from the exiled Hutchinson family. Thomas Jr.'s brother, John, took over the business. He was in charge when the large granite stores still standing today were built on Lewis's Wharf. Another relative, Samuel, who owned a store near Faneuil Hall selling "American Manufactures," worked with Robert Gould Shaw to develop the area around Lewis's Wharf in the late 1820s and 1830s. Under their leadership, Lewis Street was laid out to better connect Lewis's Wharf to North Street. The name "Lewis Street" is another lasting tribute to a successful local family.

Samuel Shaw

Samuel Shaw's father, Francis, was a very successful North End merchant, and he no doubt greatly influenced his son in commercial matters. Francis was born in Boston and later owned a home near Paul Revere, where Samuel grew up. Francis Shaw was well acquainted with another North End merchant named Robert Gould, who operated a store on Salem Street, near Prince Street. Gould also ran a "pearl works" near the mills on the northeastern edge of the Mill Pond. He contended that pearl ash was a superior ingredient for making soap and sold it in the neighborhood. In 1764, Francis Shaw and Gould invested in land in eastern Maine and sent Francis Shaw Jr., Samuel's brother, to Goudlsboro as their agent a few years later. The area was called Gouldsboro after Robert Gould. The Revolutionary War interrupted progress on this investment, as Francis Jr. led a militia company based in Gouldsboro. In addition, Gould himself died during the war. He is remembered in the name of the town, which is located near Bar Harbor and Acadia National Park, and in the name of one of Francis Jr.'s sons, Robert Gould Shaw, a major North End businessman of the nineteenth century.

Samuel and Francis Jr. grew up in North Square and attended the North Writing School with their brothers. In 1775, at the age of twenty-one, Samuel enlisted in Washington's army at Cambridge and rose to the rank of captain within five years. He continued to serve throughout the war, mostly in administrative positions, notably as aide-de-camp to General Henry Knox, also a Boston native. Shaw was present at several major battles, including Yorktown, and at the close of the Revolution he was one of the founders of the Society of the Cincinnati, a hereditary organization of American and French officers in the war. After the war, in 1784, he sailed for China aboard a New York ship called the *Empress of China*, the first American ship to reach Canton. Thus, Samuel Shaw was one of the first Americans to explore this major Chinese trading center. Shaw and the others sold ginseng, pelts and other American products and purchased tea, silk and additional highly prized Chinese commodities. They returned to New York in May 1785, inaugurating America's "China Trade," which brought great wealth to Bostonians and others for over sixty years.

Samuel Shaw used his family wealth and Revolutionary War connections to open a new trade route for American merchants. However, his brother, Francis Jr., died about a month before Samuel Shaw returned from his first trip to China. Francis Jr. left behind his two young sons, and Samuel brought them to Boston to raise himself. The following year, the young U.S. government appointed Samuel Shaw consul at Canton, where he advised American merchants on Chinese commercial regulations. Shaw was subsequently reappointed as consul by his old comrade President George Washington. As his personal wealth grew, Shaw expanded his own trade to include Macao and Bombay. It was on a subsequent trip to Bombay when Shaw became ill. Unable to find a cure there or in China, he decided to return to the United States, but he died en route in 1794 and was buried at sea near the Cape of Good Hope. More than fifty years later, Robert Gould Shaw memorialized the uncle who raised him with an obelisk in Copp's Hill Burying Ground in his native North End.

William Tudor

While Paul Revere invested in local manufacturing and Thomas Lewis and Samuel Shaw participated in international trade in the early years of

The Shaw Monument in Copp's Hill Burying Ground.

the new republic, fellow North Ender William Tudor invested his money in Boston's infrastructure. Born in 1750, Tudor grew up in North Square, attended the North Writing School and joined the army in 1775, just like his friend Samuel Shaw. Prior to his military service, however, Tudor attended Harvard, read law in the office of John Adams and opened his own practice in Boston. Due to his education and legal background, Tudor was appointed the first judge advocate general of the army with the rank of lieutenant colonel. He returned to civilian life in 1778, got married, expanded his legal practice and performed the eighth annual Boston Massacre memorial oration—a high honor. He also served as judge in the court-martial of his former neighbor, Paul Revere.

Tudor's father, John, was actually born in England. His mother moved him to Boston in 1715, the same year that Apollos Rivoire arrived in the town. They were two of the many immigrants moving to the North End during that time. John was originally an Anglican, and he later married at Christ Church. John was in "the Bakeing Business," according to his diary, and after leaving Christ Church, he joined the Second Church, where he became a deacon. John kept all of the most valuable church records, in addition to serving as the treasurer for about forty-two years, and was considered a pillar of the church all of his life. John Tudor was on the committee that commissioned Paul Revere to recast the church bell and was friends with his fellow deacon Thomas Lewis. In fact, two of the three witnesses to Tudor's will were Lewis and his son of the same name. Due to his father's activities, William Tudor was raised in the Second Church and was well acquainted with the other North End entrepreneurs.

Tudor invested in the first bridge that would connect downtown Boston to the mainland. The Charles River Bridge opened in 1786 as a replacement for the old ferry that had been operating between the North End and Charlestown for over 150 years. The successful bridge was an extension of Prince Street, which led to the heart of the bustling North End, and became a much busier thoroughfare with the increased bridge traffic. The tolls collected on the bridge made its investors even wealthier, and Tudor used some of his wealth to found the Massachusetts Historical Society, which held its first meeting in his home near Beacon Hill. Tudor was elected to both the Massachusetts House of Representatives and Senate, where he served with Harrison Gray Otis. A major force behind the Charles River Bridge, Otis induced Tudor to purchase land in the mostly unpopulated South Boston and build a bridge from there to Boston proper. The South Boston venture proved to be a failure, but Otis had other ideas. The area between the West End and the North End, which was the Mill Pond, was chosen as the next site for redevelopment, and this resulted in a major land-making project in the North End.

The Mill Pond

Privately owned mills had been operating on the publicly owned Mill Pond since 1643 under a patent provided by the town. The selectmen continually renewed and extended the patent over the course of 150 years. John Tudor was a proprietor of the Mill Pond, and William Tudor inherited his interests in the land and its enterprises. Tudor was in the Massachusetts Senate when the proprietors of the Mill Pond met in 1801 to contemplate redeveloping the area. Harrison Gray Otis joined him in the senate the following year and led other investors in mobilizing public opinion behind filling the pond. During that time, Charles Bulfinch was the chairman of Boston's board of selectmen and a well-placed ally. Bulfinch, Otis, Tudor and others blurred the line between public service and private profit, a line that was fairly unclear to begin with.

The politician-investors claimed that public health was the reason that the pond must be filled. In fact, the Mill Pond was heavily polluted. In 1804, the following conditions existed: there were "above 90 privies" and a great number of common sewers emptying into the Mill Pond, as well as "unwholesome drainings" of sugarhouses and the "fetid returns" of several distilleries and breweries still operating on the pond; the margin of the pond was "at all times covered with the putrid bodies of dogs, cats, and other animals" that were apparently dumped there by local custom; and a "vast quantity of lumber" and other dangerous debris protruded from the mud around the edges of the pond. A North Ender named Josiah Snelling, along with sixty-two other people, petitioned against filling the pond, alleging that it could easily be cleaned. Snelling's letter noted that the proprietors themselves had closed the West Boston floodgates, causing the water to stop circulating and thus become stagnant. Snelling argued that the town should clear the pond of debris, reopen the floodgates and enforce existing cleanliness rules.

Snelling and his fellow petitioners also argued that local residents were accustomed to healthy breezes from the pond in the summertime, an attractive aspect of property ownership in the greater Prince Street area. They also made a plea on behalf of the "poorer" people of the area, who benefited from the small quantities of flour and other products available from the remaining mills. The same items would be priced higher if they were not made locally. The selectmen, led by Bulfinch, created a committee to study the Mill Pond issue, and the committee quickly and unsurprisingly recommended filling the pond. The proprietors of the Mill Pond reconstituted themselves as the Boston Mill Corporation (BMC) and proceeded with the project. The Town of Boston would receive one-eighth of the new land, as well as all of the streets. Bulfinch drew up the plan for the new area himself.

Josiah Snelling Jr. (1782–1828), the most famous member of that old North End family, was born on the Snelling estate on Salem Street, near Hull Street. Josiah Snelling joined the military and fought in the War of 1812, later rising to the rank of colonel. Snelling Place in the North End is named for his family, and Fort Snelling in Minnesota is named after the colonel, who oversaw its construction. *Private collection.*

By the end of 1807, the BMC had finished the first new road through the old Mill Pond—Endicott Street, known then as Pond Street. Pond Street was a better and more direct connection between the Charles River Bridge and the Faneuil Hall area. North Margin Street was completed by the end of 1809, but it was about another five years before Thacher, Cooper and Stillman Streets reached Pond Street. These cross streets were slowly filled east to west out of the North End, finally reaching North Washington Street by 1822. Beyond the Pond Street portion of the project, which constituted an addition to the North End, most of the new land in the former Mill Pond fit neatly into a large, inverted triangle formed by Causeway, North Washington

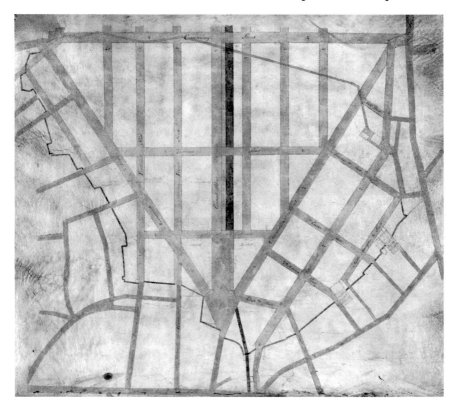

The Mill Pond plan. Charles Bulfinch (1763–1844) designed this street plan connecting the West and North Ends over the filled pond. The new land and streets were sensitively woven into the existing fabric of the town. The preexisting Prince and Salem Streets in the North End can be seen at the right of the map. *Map Reproduction Courtesy of the Norman B. Leventhal Map Center at the Boston Public Library.*

and Merrimac Streets. The entire project from the North End to the West End drew to a close in the summer of 1828, after over twenty years of work. By the time the project was finished, Charles Bulfinch had been appointed to work at the U.S. Capitol, Harrison Gray Otis had been elected mayor of Boston and William Tudor had been deceased for nearly a decade.

Legacies

Revere, Lewis, Shaw and Tudor were well positioned to build on the Revolution and expand the health and wealth of the new United States. They relied on the local network formed around North Square, the North

Writing School and the Second Church. These shared experiences kept them grounded in the North End and allowed them to share information, discuss investments and support and rely on one another in their efforts to abandon their colonial dependency on England. Paul Revere was a master craftsman, like his father, and an excellent organizer. He reached out to the federal government, as well as businessmen at home and in other states, to support his efforts to expand American manufacturing capacity. Investors and politicians knew well that they could count on Revere to learn new industrial techniques and to satisfy anyone who backed him. Thomas Lewis was a clever businessman with a commanding knowledge of maritime commerce, and he chose the best products to buy and carry in the Caribbean Sea and along the Atlantic coast. He made sure that Bostonians would continue to have a wide selection of goods even though England attempted to block traditional trade routes to American vessels after the Revolution.

Samuel Shaw was a gifted writer and administrator, and he honed those skills in the army. He was also a brave man, not only because of his service at Princeton, Brandywine, Yorktown and other battles, but also because he was willing to travel across the globe to explore Canton. Shaw was a pioneer, and his Chinese journals guided those who followed him. William Tudor's abilities as an attorney served him well as he developed the army's first criminal code. Tudor preferred a gentleman's life of politics, travel and charitable pursuits, though, and he chose mainly to invest in local projects. His financial backing allowed others to physically expand the North End, as well as other parts of Boston, notably by filling the Mill Pond and building downtown Boston's first bridge. Tudor also co-founded and supported the Massachusetts Historical Society, which continues to safeguard the letters of Patriots like Paul Revere and dozens of other North Enders.

Revere, Lewis, Shaw and Tudor were all gone by 1819, and as their children and grandchildren built on the successes of the previous generations, they eventually moved out of the North End. By the 1820s, most of the people who remained in the neighborhood, as well as those who began to move in, worked in the shipyards or related industries; labored in the many construction projects, including new land, bridges and streets; or ran the many taverns and shops that catered to the local population. At two hundred years old, the North End no longer had a large upper class, and more sailors and immigrants could afford to live in the growing neighborhood.

CHAPTER 8

THE OLD COCKEREL

A New North End Emerges in Its Third Century

When the North End turned two hundred years old, the Second Church building was the oldest in Boston. When it was constructed in 1721, it was known as the New Brick Meeting House, and a weather vane in the shape of a six-foot rooster, commonly referred to as a cockerel, was placed at the top of the tall steeple. Built as a congregational meetinghouse, New Brick was known as the Second Church after its merger with the original Old North during the Revolution. By 1830, the once young rooster had been surveying the neighborhood for over a century. From his vantage point, he had watched thousands of ships come and go from all parts of the world. He saw the construction of many of those ships in the North End shipyards. He watched as the infant Paul Revere was carried to his church for baptism, and he was watching forty years later when the Patriot set out from North Square to alarm the countryside. He lived through his own church joining the Unitarian movement, and he watched the decline of the old Hutchinson mansion as it was subdivided and finally torn down as the demographics of the neighborhood continued to change. If we use this point of view high above the streets of the North End, we can see the completed developments and changes in process at the beginning of the neighborhood's third century.

A New Market District

Even though Faneuil Hall had been enlarged in 1805, the merchant-investors of Boston, who were quickly resettling themselves onto Beacon Hill, made sure that a "market square" was part of the Mill Pond project a few years later. Apparently, many of the same individuals were still concerned about adequate market space in the 1820s, and the expansion of the Faneuil Hall

This cockerel weather vane watched over generations of North Enders. *Private collection.*

market area was the result. Part of the Faneuil Hall project included the creation of Commercial Street, which was laid out in a straight line from the "stores on Long wharf" up to the new market building, now known as Quincy Market. The new street was referred to as "a street to the Long Wharf, for the general accommodation of the citizens, and particularly of those in the North section of the city." At that time it had not yet been extended into the North End, but a group of leading merchants, including Robert G. Shaw and Samuel S. Lewis, designed the North End portion of Commercial Street, from the new market all the way up to Battery Street. Shaw and Lewis had a particular interest in the project because they owned the flats and wharves over which Commercial Street, and later Fulton, was to be built. They incorporated themselves as the Mercantile Wharf Corporation to complete the job, and between 1827 and 1833, they created

The Faneuil Hall market extension, 1827. This is the earliest known image of the new buildings. The strip of land in the foreground, in front of the three new buildings, is the beginning of Commercial Street. *Courtesy of the Boston Public Library, Print Department.*

Commercial, Fulton and Lewis Streets as a new market district for the North End (Atlantic Avenue was not built until 1870). Commercial Street received its name because it provided North Enders with direct access not only to Long Wharf but also to the many stores and wharves in the South End. Lewis Street was named for Lewis Wharf, where Thomas Lewis's son John was still the wharfinger. Fulton Street was most likely named after Robert Fulton, who is credited with creating the first commercially successful steamboats. Although there are streets and counties named after Fulton across the country, he did have a North End connection—the copper boilers for his early ships were manufactured by Paul Revere.

The Black Sea

The old rooster did not have to look far behind his own meetinghouse to see the area around Fulton Street, including smaller lanes that sprung up to connect it to Commercial and North Streets, quickly fill with stores. In fact, Fulton Street was described by Robert G. Shaw and others in 1841 as "an easy and commodious thorough fare…a large amount of trade is there carried on, and in [its] stores a great quantity of valuable merchandise is deposited."

Unfortunately, Shaw's description was part of a petition for more lamps on Fulton Street because "of late, four or five burglaries have been committed therein and a considerable quantity of merchandise abstracted." One of the reasons for the increase in theft was that a part of North Street, between Union and Richmond, had devolved into a red-light district known as the Black Sea. By the early 1840s, the dance halls, gaming houses, brothels, bars and violent crimes in the Black Sea were so numerous and dangerous that many Bostonians feared the North End in general. However, a steady stream of sailors, travelers and suburban men kept the area in business. As Boston's state representative said in session in 1853, "Who ever heard of a Boston boy being shook down in [North] Street?" The Black Sea catered to a clientele with no real roots in the neighborhood, and this posed a problem for merchants and residents alike.

The rest of North Street, above North Square, had been greatly improved with stores and businesses. In addition, the reputable part of North Street was adjacent to the Fulton Street commercial area, which extended to Quincy Market, not even fifteen years old when the Black Sea was already firmly established. The proximity to the active waterfront, the low socioeconomic status of the neighborhood and the fact that the red-light district had recently been chased off of Beacon Hill by Mayor Josiah Quincy seem to have been enough to help plant the Black Sea in the North End. The area was so bad that in April 1851, 144 people were arrested in one night. While nearly 100 of those people were prostitutes, 33 of them were taken into custody for running "houses of ill fame" and violating noise and license laws. The city responded weakly to this kind of activity. It does not appear that officials curtailed the number of liquor licenses distributed, but they did decide to rename the street in an attempt to change its reputation. North Street had actually been called Ann Street since 1708, but the city council decided to rename the stretch of Ann Street that ran through the Black Sea "North Street" in 1852.

Protestant Reformers

As urban areas across the United States swelled and places like the Black Sea multiplied, the country underwent a second "Great Awakening." This was a large, national, religious revival that caused a rise in conversion and activity in the various Protestant branches of Christianity. Thousands of people became newly engaged in social activism, which led to reform movements concerning poverty, temperance (abstaining from alcoholic beverages), prison conditions, women's rights, the abolition of slavery and public education. One successful reformer was Edward Taylor. After spending about ten years at sea, Taylor was reborn during the Second Great Awakening and became a Methodist minister. In 1828, the First Methodist Church moved to a newly constructed building on North Bennet Street, near the corner of Hanover Street, and invited Father Taylor to preach in the old building on Methodist Alley (now Hanover Avenue). His authentic knowledge of the life of a sailor, combined with his vigorous style, drew large crowds. The Methodists of Boston, who later were joined by people from other denominations, subsequently created the Port Society of Boston to help Taylor minister to the sailors in the city. They built a bethel, or church

The bethel in North Square (1833–1884), Sacred Heart Catholic Church (1884–present). The façade was updated in 1911. *Private collection.*

building, in North Square in 1833 as a permanent place to reach out to the men who worked at sea. North Square was chosen because of its proximity to the Black Sea and the wharves. Taylor's ministry in North Square and his attempts to save sailors from the local temptations lasted nearly forty years, and his abilities and genuine concern for others won him great respect from people across the city.

Religiously inspired reformers attempted to create other changes in the North End as well. For example, Christ Church and First Baptist Church had both opened Sunday schools by 1816, two of the earliest in Boston.

Christ Church ("Old North Church") on Salem Street, as seen from Hull Street, in the 1840s. *Private collection.*

Churches created Sunday schools for boys and girls of all ages, even those who were just a few years old. Their primary purpose was to teach religion, but through their curricula they also encouraged the values of discipline and industriousness. The original Sunday schools were intended for any children who needed them, especially those living in poverty. Reformers also set up "missions" in the North End in order to eliminate poverty, disease and crime. Unfortunately, many of the missionaries of the early 1820s and 1830s believed that, on some level, people affected by poverty and disease were actually the cause of those social ills and required moral guidance to overcome their individual vices, which in turn would eliminate societal problems. Though seriously concerned about living conditions in the North End, the missionaries often failed because their prejudices precluded them from getting at the root of the issues, and they offended the people they were attempting to help. Edward Taylor was an important example of a reformer who avoided these unhelpful attitudes.

The North End's First Catholic Church

The old rooster on Hanover Street had seen changes within his own church, as well as elsewhere in the North End, but he never would have imagined that a Catholic church would be established in this old Puritan neighborhood. During the 1820s, there had been only two Catholic churches in all of Boston: the Cathedral on Franklin Street and St. Augustine's Chapel in South Boston. In 1831, Bishop Benedict Fenwick began to search for a suitable site to serve the numerous Irish immigrants of the North and West Ends. Fenwick purchased four lots at the corner of Cooper and Pond Streets, where he personally supervised the construction of a new church. On May 22, 1836, Fenwick dedicated St. Mary's Church—the first Catholic church ever built in the North End.

The construction of St. Mary's was also a sign that any brief prestige attached to the former Mill Pond area had long passed. Less than a month after the church's dedication, thirty-seven people submitted a petition to the city council to change the name of Pond Street. The Protestant petitioners wanted "some other name a little more compatible with the feelings of the inhabitants of that section of the City." The petitioners narrowed their suggestions for a new name down to two: Endicott Street, after "Governor Endicott," and Putnam Street, after "Genl. Putnam." The residents of this area looked to the memory of John Endecott (spellings vary) and Israel Putnam to legitimize their section of the North End, which was a new portion of an old and historic neighborhood now

St. Mary's Church, the first Catholic church ever built in the North End, as it appeared less than a decade after its 1836 dedication. It was located on Endicott Street, at the corner of Cooper Street, until it was demolished and replaced in 1877. *Private collection.*

thronged with Catholics. The council approved the change to Endicott Street immediately. Ultimately, John Endecott was chosen because of his status as a founding Puritan of the colony. Endecott had actually settled in Massachusetts before John Winthrop and his associates ever arrived on its shores. Officially, Endecott had been governor before Winthrop. Endecott was governor of Massachusetts five times, and he was governor or deputy governor continuously from 1649 until shortly before his death in 1665. As governor, he had established the first mint in Massachusetts, placing John Hull in charge. The colony generally flourished under his leadership, though he was intolerant of religious dissenters, especially Quakers, and aggressive toward Native Americans.

John Endecott (circa 1588–1665), circa 1665. *Courtesy of the Commonwealth of Massachusetts, Art Commission.*

The Creation of the Slum

Even before the terrible famine years, large numbers of Irish immigrants settled in Boston, and the new St. Mary's Church was quickly overwhelmed. In 1843, the Catholic Diocese purchased a warehouse on Moon Street and converted it for use as a church. It was dedicated as St. John the Baptist Church, and it was almost instantly filled with worshipers. By 1850, Boston's population was nearly 140,000, more than double what it had been when Father Taylor opened his bethel, and almost half of the residents were foreign born, including 46,000 people from Ireland. Boston's waterfront streets were inhabited by Irish immigrants, and in the North End in 1850, Irish people were concentrated in the area around St. Mary's Church on Endicott Street, as well as around St. John's in North Square and all the way up North Street to the former site of the North Battery, which had been dismantled after the Revolution. The neighborhood's tiny, dead-end "courts" and "places"—once the spaces between buildings—were soon filled with wooden dwellings to house the Irish immigrants.

According to the historian Oscar Handlin, old mansions and unused warehouses were subdivided into "dreary tenement houses" that lacked "conveniences or sanitation" and featured a "general inflammability." The grounds around formerly fashionable residences and "the hitherto unusable sites created by the city's irregular streets" were filled with hastily constructed tenements. Landlords filled "every vacant spot, behind, beside, or within an

The Endicott School was built in 1840 on Cooper Street, near St. Mary's Church, to accommodate the expanding population of the North End. The need for public education grew so rapidly that the city was already planning an addition in 1849. The Endicott School was coeducational during the 1800s. *Private collection.*

Henchman Street, circa 1893. These eighteenth-century wooden houses are typical of
the housing stock that was available for the Irish immigrants in the mid-1800s. At the
corner of Commercial Street, to the right of the image, is a more substantial apartment
building of the type commonly built in the neighborhood between the 1890s and 1920s.
In the background, across Commercial Street, is an older town house that was constructed
between 1800 and 1830. *Courtesy of the Boston Public Library, Print Department.*

old structure…exploiting the last iota of space" in the North End. Smallpox,
cholera and tuberculosis spread throughout the filthy slums created for the
Irish people, as did crime, alcohol and prostitution. Under these conditions,
according to Handlin, the Irish were "hastened in the midst of life to death."
After the famine began, however, Irish immigrants arrived in such large
numbers that they soon moved into the center of the North End and on to
Copp's Hill. Irish North Enders lived in a neighborhood overwhelmed with
people, surrounded by industry and patrolled by Yankee missionaries.

Charlotte Saunders Cushman

One of the parishioners at the old rooster's church became America's first
international theatre star. Charlotte Cushman was born on Parmenter Street
in 1816, and she joined the Second Church in 1829, when Ralph Waldo
Emerson, the future writer and transcendentalist, was minister. Cushman
sang in the church choir and made an unsuccessful attempt at a professional

One of the ancient buildings that awaited Irish immigrants, located at the corner of Lewis and North Streets. Lewis Street is in the foreground, and North Street is at the left of this late 1800s image. Despite the generally shabby appearance of the building, including several broken windows, the proprietor is dressed in a fine suit and top hat for the photograph. The Piccolo Nido restaurant is on this site today. *Courtesy of the Boston Public Library, Print Department.*

singing career. She turned to acting and was so successful in America and England that she was able to move to an enormous home in Rome by the time she was thirty-six years old. Cushman's Italian home was a center for writers and artists, especially women, including the pioneering sculptors Harriet Hosmer, Edmonia Lewis and Emma Stebbins. Cushman, who was a lesbian, returned to Boston with Stebbins, her partner, in time for the dedication of a new school built on her Parmenter Street birthplace. The first school ever named after a woman in Boston, the Charlotte Cushman School officially opened early in 1872. Cushman herself came to the school to address the students and perform some of her most popular pieces. She felt great pride that this honor had been bestowed upon a woman and an actress, and she wrote, "Nothing in all my life has so pleased me as this." Charlotte Cushman died of cancer in 1876. Her funeral at King's Chapel

Charlotte Cushman (1816–1876) of Parmenter Street, 1830s. This portrait is hanging in the Charlotte Cushman Room in the Boston Public Library at Copley Square. *Courtesy of the Boston Public Library, Print Department.*

was filled with fans and dignitaries, and the Cushman School was draped in mourning. Cushman left money and property from her vast estate to her family, friends and Stebbins. Most of her obituaries assumed that the great actress would never be forgotten, but her memory had faded by the end of the century. In the early 1900s, however, a number of Charlotte Cushman Clubs were opened as safe places for young actresses to stay while performing in various American cities. Cushman was buried at Mount Auburn Cemetery in Cambridge, and the Hanover Street rooster who watched her grow up in the North End made the trip to Cambridge to see her laid to rest.

The Second Church Leaves the Neighborhood

Below the rooster's perch, the building of the Second Church was in almost constant need of repairs. In 1819–1820, the congregation had expended money to remove the original box pews and replace them with the longer benches more familiar to churchgoers today. In 1823, it had the steeple rebuilt because it was in a "decayed and dangerous condition." In 1832, the congregation sold its land adjacent to the church, along Richmond Street, to finance $3,000 worth of additional repairs. By then, a significant portion of the members were advocating for the construction of a new church. A large and wealthy segment of the congregation had already moved out of the North End, and these members felt that the time was right to build a new church on Somerset Street, in the Beacon Hill neighborhood. This new location would be convenient for people who continued to live in the North End, as well as for those who had moved away but retained membership and commuted for worship on Hanover Street.

Boston's city council forced the issue in the early 1840s by telling the congregation that it had to either extensively repair the building or take it down. The congregation could have sold the building to the Catholic Diocese of Boston, which offered to purchase the church for $19,000 for its own burgeoning community, but the Second Church refused the offer and rejected the idea of moving to Beacon Hill. Chandler Robbins, minister at the church since 1833, noted that the portion of the congregation that still resided in the North End in the 1840s resisted relocation "with great firmness." March 10, 1844, was the "last day for public worship in that building," which had served its congregation for 123 years. Robbins was determined that the church building "shall not fall unhonored." He said that "this old pile shall not be swept away forever from the sight of men, without a becoming commemoration of its long and interesting history." Robbins recounted the history in great detail and then preached on the progress that society had made "since the corner-stone of this edifice was laid."

The church's pulpit, pews, organ and bell were purchased by churches in the vicinity of Boston. The aging church was dismembered, and people from across the city watched the unusual spectacle. On May 30, as the

The Second Church on Hanover Street as it appeared when it was taken down in 1844. Note Shem Drowne's rooster atop the spire. *Private collection.*

cornerstone of the new church was put in place, Robbins said that he and the congregation "never realized how strong and tender were the associations that bound it [the old church] to our hearts, till we saw it dismantled, desolate, and ruinous, whilst the work of its destruction was going on." Yet, he hoped that the new building would stand for centuries "and be suited to the wants and tastes not only of ourselves but our children." The ornate and costly new building of the Second Church reopened in 1845 with the old brass rooster atop the steeple. Unfortunately, the congregation took on a large debt to construct such a beautiful building, and its ability to pay the bills greatly diminished.

Second Church (1845–1849), First Methodist Church (1849–1870), as seen circa 1865 on Hanover Street, near the corner of Richmond Street. *Courtesy of the Bostonian Society/Old State House, Boston Streets Photograph Collection, circa 1865–1999.*

Due to financial problems, swift and unprecedented demographic changes and the spreading Black Sea, the congregation of the Second Church was forced to sell its new building, which it hadn't even used for five years. The congregation moved to the South End in 1849, and after 200 years, the Second Church left the neighborhood it had helped to create. Unlike most other North Enders of English descent, the old rooster stayed behind. The First Methodist Church purchased the building for less than half its original cost, but the rooster continued to dutifully stand watch for two more decades. A hurricane hit Boston in September 1869, and as the historian

The First Methodist Church after the hurricane of September 1869. The church was demolished in 1870 and replaced by Cockerel Hall, located at 287–289 Hanover Street. *Courtesy of the Boston Public Library, Print Department.*

The old North End rooster, created in 1721, watches the sunset from his perch atop the First Church in Cambridge, Congregational, where he has been since 1873. The church faces the location on Cambridge Common where General George Washington first took command of the Continental army on July 3, 1775. Harvard Yard is in the center of the image, and from there rises the steeple of Memorial Church, built in 1932, which closely resembles that of the Old North Church. The Boston skyline is in the background.

Edwin Bacon described the scene, the rooster was knocked from the steeple and "astonished a family near by, by coming uninvited into its house to tea." The weather vane was repaired but was not returned to its perch because the hurricane had also knocked down the steeple. Already seriously damaged, the rest of the building was demolished due to the widening of Hanover Street the following year. A new multiuse building was constructed and opened at what is today 287–289 Hanover Street, and it was called Cockerel Hall in honor of the original weather vane rooster that had watched over the North End on this spot for almost 150 years. Like the bell cast by Paul Revere for the same church, the rooster moved to Cambridge, where he still resides.

When the North End began its third century under the watchful eye of the cockerel, the Irish residents were but one component of its diverse population. Due to the Catholic faith of the Irish, other, more established Bostonians generally tried to keep them from positions of power and responsibility in business and politics. By the 1850s, however, Irish North Enders could no longer be held back.

CHAPTER 9

THE IRISH ASCENSION

From the Eliot School Case to the Civil War

During the 1850s, tensions continued to build between the native Protestant and immigrant Catholic communities in Boston. At the end of the decade, those tensions exploded in an incident at the Eliot School in the North End. In a deliberate effort to instill Protestant values, the Boston School Committee's regulations in the 1850s required the reading of the Protestant Bible and various prayers in the classroom each morning, as well as the recitation of the Lord's Prayer in the Protestant fashion. Despite the fact that the words used in both the Catholic and Protestant versions of these prayers were nearly identical, the spirit of the words and the alteration of just a few had tremendous meaning for both sets of Christians. Fortunately, the staff members of the Eliot School were sensitive enough to this conflict and to the needs of their students that they allowed the Catholic boys to either mumble their own prayers or remain silent while the teacher and the Protestant students recited each morning.

The majority of the North End's newer residents were Irish Catholics, and though St. Mary's Church had already opened a school for girls, most of the boys within the parish attended the Eliot School on Tileston Street. On Monday, March 7, 1859, a teacher at the school named Sophia Shepard asked a young Catholic boy named Thomas Whall to recite the biblical Ten Commandments for the class, obviously in the Protestant version. Whall, who was ten years old, refused. Changing its regular practice, the school administration had asked Shepard to enforce the rules regarding prayers. The following Monday, she again called upon young Whall to recite the Ten Commandments, and again he refused. The assistant principal, McLaurin Cooke, then entered the classroom and beat the student into bloody unconsciousness. Samuel Mason, the principal, announced that day that any boys who refused to recite the Protestant Ten Commandments would be

The Eliot School, on the corner of North Bennet and Wiggin Streets, as it appeared between 1837 and 1859. This was the site of the case of Thomas Whall. The Eliot School was a boys' school for most of the 1800s. *Private collection.*

immediately expelled, causing the dismissal of about four hundred Catholic boys that week. The boys were by some accounts encouraged, and by others threatened, by their priest, Father Bernardine Wiget of St. Mary's, to refuse to recite any non-Catholic prayers.

Father Wiget

Father Bernardine Wiget was from the Swiss canton, or state, called Schwyz. A brief civil war had erupted in 1847 between Catholic and Protestant cantons. Wiget had been studying at the Jesuit seminary in Fribourg, and that canton, like Schwyz, was aligned with the Catholic forces. The Protestant armies defeated the Catholics and attacked the seminary. Wiget and others disguised themselves and escaped. The Jesuit leadership ordered dozens of priests, including Wiget, to leave Switzerland for the United States. Wiget spent some time in Maryland, where he founded a school for boys at St. Ignatius Church, in Port Tobacco, in 1855. He was assigned to St. Mary's Church in the North End the following year and immediately formed a sodality, or youth group, for boys. Thomas Whall and hundreds of other Catholic boys in the parish joined the sodality. Because of his own experiences, Wiget urged Catholics in America to strongly assert their faith in the face of discrimination. With the expulsion of about half of the students at the Eliot School in March 1859, Wiget immediately formed a boys' school under the auspices of St. Mary's.

Bernardine Wiget (circa 1820–1883) of Endicott Street, the champion of Boston's Catholic schools. *Courtesy of the Woodstock College Archives, Special Collections, Georgetown University Library.*

Thomas Whall's parents sued Assistant Principal Cooke for beating their son. Henry F. Durant, the future founder of Wellesley College, defended Cooke. He didn't argue about the severity of the beating but rather focused on the right of school officials to administer beatings as they saw fit. Durant claimed that Wiget coerced the Catholic children with "the exercise of a dark and…fearfully dangerous power." He asked the court, "Who is this priest who comes here from a foreign land to instruct us in our laws?" Durant stated that either the laws of Massachusetts would be enforced or "a Jesuit can dictate from Endicott Street as to the management of our public schools." The lawyer was clearly playing on the fears of a papist conspiracy, and he constantly asserted that this was "our" state and "our" school—meaning Anglo-Americans and no one else. Durant won his case, and Cooke was

New North on Hanover Street, at the corner of Clark Street, dedicated in 1804. *Private collection.*

acquitted. The pastor of the New North Meeting House at that time was Arthur Buckminster Fuller, brother of the feminist and journalist Margaret Fuller. Arthur Fuller was pleased by Cooke's acquittal, and he, along with other leading ministers, acquired, published and distributed Durant's Eliot School case argument to encourage Protestant officials in their openly anti-Catholic methods.

Aftermath

Within a short time, life inside the Eliot School seemed to have returned to pre-1859 normalcy, mostly because the school committee amended its regulations after the controversy, and only teachers were required to recite the prayers. Of course, both the remaining students and Miss Shepard were probably craving stability and an end to the strife. Changing the rules was a compromise at best—the schools would continue to administer with a Protestant outlook. Wiget's school at St. Mary's continued to grow, and he is remembered as the founder of parochial schools in Boston. Unlike Mason and Cooke at the Eliot School, who lived in Chelsea, and the attorney Durant, who made his home on Beacon Hill, Wiget actually dwelled in the North End. As a local resident, and a priest, he had more influence in the community, and he used his power to save the minds and souls of North End children. Wiget was too controversial for Boston, however, and in 1860, Bishop John Fitzpatrick transferred him to Baltimore. He appeared in the news again a few years later after the assassination of President Lincoln. One of the conspirators in the assassination plot was a Maryland woman named Mary Surratt. She earned the dubious distinction of being the first woman executed by the United States government, and it was Wiget who administered her "last rites" and accompanied her to the gallows.

Bernardine Wiget died at St. Ignatius Church in Port Tobacco shortly after New Year's Day 1883. His memory continued to be cherished in Boston, and about a decade after his death, an opportunity to memorialize him presented itself. North Margin Street, completed in 1809, originally turned at the First Baptist Church and ended at Salem Street. In 1892, North Margin was extended all the way to Stillman Street, leaving a small alley between Salem and North Margin, which the city dubbed Wiget Street. Hundreds of former students at the school he had founded at St. Mary's gathered at Faneuil Hall on the fortieth anniversary of the Eliot School case. The toastmaster was Thomas Whall's brother, William. One of the many speakers he introduced was former congressman Patrick Collins, who would later be elected the second Irish-born mayor of Boston. Collins lived in Chelsea as a boy, but he was a Sunday school teacher at St. Mary's School. He, like almost everyone else who spoke that night, remembered Wiget fondly as an educator who had helped build the character of the boys in his care.

Arthur Fuller, who lived on Hull Street, was considered a leading progressive in the Unitarian movement. During the Eliot School case, however, he represented the nativist reaction to the Irish immigrants. Fuller left New North after the controversy and accepted a position as minister at the First (Unitarian) Parish in Watertown, where there were far fewer Irish Catholics. In 1862, the Catholic Diocese purchased New North and rededicated it as St. Stephen's Catholic Church. During the Civil War, Fuller resigned his position in Watertown and became the chaplain for the Sixteenth Massachusetts Volunteer Infantry. However, in December 1862, the Nineteenth Massachusetts was under heavy fire at Fredericksburg, Virginia, and Fuller volunteered to pick up a weapon and defend the position. He was killed in the battle, fought only about fifty miles away from Port Tobacco, Maryland, where Father Wiget would spend his final days. Fuller did not have to fight, but he felt that it was his duty as a Christian, and he died a Patriot. Fuller's North End neighbor Thomas Cass, a member of the Boston School Committee during the Eliot School case, also gave his life for his country during the Civil War.

The Irish Ninth

Thomas Cass was born in Ireland, but his family relocated to the North End when he was still a child. Cass worshiped at St. Mary's, and he must have been sympathetic to the plight of the young Irish boys at the Eliot School. It may have been his influence that caused the school committee to change the regulations about forcing Catholics to recite Protestant prayers. Prior to the controversy, Cass, who lived on North Bennet Street, was the leader of a Boston militia company called the Columbian Artillery. In 1854, Cass's company, which was almost entirely Irish, was a part of the military force assigned to guard the extradition of Anthony Burns, an African-American man being returned to slavery in Virginia under a federal law. Participating in the Burns case did not win Cass any friends in Boston, the country's antislavery center, and it was not long before the Columbian Artillery was forced to disband. However, when the Civil War began in April 1861, Cass gathered the core of his old company and successfully recruited enough men to fill an entire regiment, the Ninth Massachusetts. Colonel Cass commanded

CAUTION!!

COLORED PEOPLE

OF BOSTON, ONE & ALL,

You are hereby respectfully CAUTIONED and advised, to avoid conversing with the

Watchmen and Police Officers of Boston,

For since the recent ORDER OF THE MAYOR & ALDERMEN, they are empowered to act as

KIDNAPPERS

AND

Slave Catchers,

And they have already been actually employed in KIDNAPPING, CATCHING, AND KEEPING SLAVES. Therefore, if you value your LIBERTY, and the *Welfare of the Fugitives* among you, *Shun* them in every possible manner, as so many *HOUNDS* on the track of the most unfortunate of your race.

Keep a Sharp Look Out for KIDNAPPERS, and have TOP EYE open.

APRIL 24, 1851.

African Americans in the North were being kidnapped and sold into slavery in the South. African Americans living or working in the North End were warned to avoid policemen, who could assist the kidnappers with impunity under an 1850 federal law, which was used to arrest the formerly enslaved Anthony Burns. *Courtesy of the Museum of African American History, Boston, Massachusetts.*

the "Irish Ninth" until he was mortally wounded in July 1862 at the Battle of Malvern Hill, Virginia. He returned to the North End, where he succumbed to his wounds on July 12. Cass was buried in Cambridge, but there is a statue of this famous North Ender in the Boston Public Garden. Colonel Cass and his fellow Irish Americans proved their patriotism during the Civil War, just like nearly 200,000 African Americans who fought for their country and their freedom.

The Fifty-fourth Massachusetts

The creation of the Fifty-fourth Massachusetts, the first regiment of African Americans from the North, brought together two strands of North End history. Boston's earliest settlement of African Americans was in the North End, and over the years, many residents of that area on Copp's Hill fought hard for their own freedom and civil rights. The Fifty-fourth Massachusetts achieved national fame, and the valor of those men deeply changed public opinion in the country, winning a victory for equality. President Lincoln's administration required African-American regiments to be under the command of white officers. As is well known, the Fifty-fourth Massachusetts was placed under the command of Robert Gould Shaw, himself already a veteran of the war. On May 28, 1863, the Fifty-fourth traveled to downtown Boston from its training camp in the Readville section of Hyde Park. The men paraded through the city and were reviewed by Governor John Andrew on the common.

After a brief recess to say goodbye to family members and friends, the regiment formed into companies and continued its march. The soldiers left the common and proceeded to State Street, from which they turned onto Commercial Street and marched into the North End. They reached Battery Wharf a little before one o'clock and, after a couple of hours, had loaded all of their horses and equipment onto the ship that would take them to South Carolina. Frederick Douglass, whose son, Lewis, was in the regiment, walked around the wharf to encourage the soldiers as they left for war. Colonel Shaw remembered that day as one of pride and hope for him and his fellow soldiers. Shaw had been named after his grandfather, Robert Gould Shaw, the leading nineteenth-century merchant who was the grandson of Francis and Sarah Shaw of North Square. Robert Shaw the elder's wealth allowed his own son and daughter-in-law to become philanthropists and abolitionists, causes that directly influenced the choice of their son, Colonel Shaw, as commander of the Fifty-fourth. When the Fifty-fourth Massachusetts marched through the

North End in 1863, many Irish residents of the neighborhood had already died in the Civil War. Their patriotism as soldiers had helped to ameliorate some of the prejudices held against the Irish, and their staunch assertiveness in religious affairs helped the Catholic hierarchy expand the number of churches and schools in the community.

The Golden Age

According to the official history of the Catholic Archdiocese of Boston, the 1860s and 1870s was the "golden age" for Irish Catholics in the North End because of the improvements made in the Catholic infrastructure. In less than a decade after it opened, St. Stephen's was enlarged, as well as "raised upon a basement," to accommodate another church below the main sanctuary. The original St. Mary's on Endicott Street was torn down, and a massive, ornate new building was dedicated on December 16, 1877. Catholics from

St. Stephen's Church in the 1920s. The building was raised about six feet in 1870, as is evidenced by the fact that the pilasters no longer reach ground level. A clock was also added to the cupola. *Courtesy of the Bostonian Society/Old State House, Boston Streets Photograph Collection, circa 1865–1999.*

First Methodist Church (1828–1849), Free-Will Baptist Church (1849–1873), St. John the Baptist Catholic Church (1873–1911) on North Bennet Street, near the corner of Hanover Street. This was the first North End church for Portuguese and Italian Catholics. The Italian portion of the congregation left and founded St. Leonard's in 1876. *Private collection.*

Portugal and Italy also took up residence in the North End. In 1873, the diocese purchased the Free-Will Baptist Church building on North Bennet Street for both national groups and rededicated it as St. John the Baptist Catholic Church. People of Irish descent dominated the Catholic hierarchy in the city and may have been insensitive to the needs of these newcomers, especially the Italian immigrants. A Portuguese priest was assigned to the church, prompting the Italians to request a church of their own. In 1876, the Italians of St. John's founded their own church, St. Leonard's, at the corner of Hanover and Prince Streets.

St. Leonard's Church on Prince Street, often locally called "St. Anthony's," is the only Catholic church building in the North End that was not originally a Protestant house of worship.

Even as the Portuguese and Italian churches formed, the Irish, or "English-speaking parishes," continued to grow. Between 1865 and 1880, the population of the North End was almost exclusively Catholic and Irish or Irish-American. After two decades as an oppressed minority in the neighborhood, the Irish assumed control of their lives and welfare. The Black Sea was shrinking, and North Enders were beginning to rebuild the run-down neighborhood. By 1880, Boston's 250th anniversary, the Baptist, Congregational and Methodist Churches were no longer based in the neighborhood, though Protestants maintained ministries for the benefit of non-Catholic sailors who rented rooms and entertained themselves in the North End. It would seem that the papist invasion envisioned by Reverend Fuller's Puritan ancestors had in some very real ways come to pass on the congested and dirty streets of the North End.

CHAPTER 10

REFORM AND MODERNIZATION

T he North End was home to many famous charitable groups in the last half of the nineteenth century. The Home for Little Wanderers was established in 1865 because of the thousands of children who were left orphaned or destitute by the Civil War. The home was based on Baldwin Place, in the vacated Second Baptist Church building (the congregation had just moved to the South End). Children were temporarily sheltered there until they were ready to move on to a new life. Very often the staff at the home found adoptive families in other parts of Massachusetts or in other states. The mostly poor residents of the North End were woefully overcrowded into dilapidated housing, and few social reformers would have considered the neighborhood a good place to raise children. The Children's Aid Society (CAS) was also founded in Boston at the close of the Civil War, and it worked primarily with children on probation or otherwise referred by the courts. Rather than being sent to jail or some other institution, the children under the charge of the CAS were sent to sewing classes, woodworking classes and reading groups and even underwent military-style drilling. While neither the CAS nor the Home for Little Wanderers was avowedly religious in nature, another organization founded at about the same time was clearly motivated by a religious fervor: the North End Mission.

By the 1870s, Protestant reformers were still interested in changing the habits of individuals, but they could no longer ignore the fact that poverty and crime had roots in societal conditions, not personal flaws. The North End Mission was organized in 1867 under the auspices of the First Methodist Church on Hanover Street, but it soon gained moral and financial backing from individuals throughout the Protestant community in Boston. The mission rented space at 201 North Street, formerly the site of a saloon, and it was not long before it purchased the entire building. Its strategy was the same

Second Baptist Church (1810–1865), Home for Little Wanderers (1865–1889), Beth Israel Synagogue (1890–1922) on Baldwin Place, as seen from Salem Street. *Private collection.*

as that of Father Taylor at the North Square bethel—you must go directly to the people you wish to help. The mission focused its attention mainly on women and children and housed a small number of people, in addition to running a Sabbath school and a nursery. It taught sewing, cooking and other domestic skills, while simultaneously discouraging the consumption of alcohol and encouraging reading, Bible study and use of the chapel within the mission.

In 1873, in order to physically remove young children from the dangers of the North End, the mission purchased a very large piece of land in what was then the separate town of West Roxbury. It called the new facility the Mount Hope Home for Children, where young people could live in a healthy environment until their parents were deemed ready

The North End Mission, 201 North Street, late 1800s. The North End Mission was located here between 1867 and 1902. Afterward, the First Italian Methodist Episcopal Church moved into the building. *Courtesy of the Boston Public Library, Print Department.*

to make homes for them. Though they may have wanted to enroll in some of the practical classes to gain valuable job skills, many North End women were scared of the possibility of losing their children and felt insulted by the low value placed on their ethnic heritage and religion. The mission conducted all of its classes, including Bible reading, in English

Teaching a young Italian girl how to read English at the North End Mission. The teacher's outfit and the furnishings of the room were meant to show young women the proper way to dress and keep house. *Courtesy of the Boston Public Library, Print Department.*

and was always affiliated with Protestant churches. While the mission helped hundreds of people, there were few Jewish or Catholic (Italian or Portuguese) participants in its programs. Located in the same place for over three decades, the mission became a widely respected model for reforming areas considered to be slums.

By the 1870s, outsiders viewed the North End as a perfect place for Protestant middle-class involvement in crime and poverty prevention. Reformers created an "industrial home" at the corner of Salem and North Bennet Streets in 1879. Like the mission, it originally focused on reaching women and children with domestic classes, hoping that many individuals would be saved. Within a few years, however, the home was reorganized into the North Bennet Street Industrial School under the leadership of a group of women reformers led by Pauline Agassiz Shaw. The Industrial School believed that society was not providing the great mass of people with the skills necessary for successful employment. An industrial education was necessary in order to compete for jobs in the industries in the North End, as well as in other parts of the Boston area. The Industrial School created classes

The chapel inside the North End Mission looked more like a train station than a Catholic church. It did not attract many Italian worshipers. *Courtesy of the Boston Public Library, Print Department.*

to appeal to the widest number of men, women and children as possible. Sewing, dressmaking, cooking, carpentry, cabinetmaking, printing, clay modeling and, by the twentieth century, radio and telegraph operating were all part of the curriculum. The school also offered recreational activities, as well as access to the on-site library, reading rooms and "coffee room," where men and boys could enjoy coffee, donuts, daily papers and games. Women could use the on-site laundry to take in wash to earn extra money, while their children stayed in the day-care center.

Public Dollars Follow Private Funding

The programs and services described thus far were privately funded efforts. In the late nineteenth century, however, the city government also began to fund improvements in the North End. Boston's government was still dominated by "Yankees," and therefore the same Anglo-Protestant, bourgeois values that

The North Bennet Street School on Salem Street, at the corner of North Bennet. This structure was built in 1885 to house the original Industrial School. This institution, which dropped the word "industrial" from its name, still operates a wide array of classes and training, including cabinetmaking, bookbinding and preservation carpentry.

motivated private or church-based social service programs also pervaded public services. For example, reading in English was seen as an important value, so the North End received its first public library branch in 1883. It was located in the Hancock School on Parmenter Street, but it was poorly ventilated and quickly became overcrowded. In the early 1890s, the library was moved to a second-floor room at 166 Hanover Street, where there was better light and air, and mischievous boys and other troublemakers had a difficult time getting in. In addition to light and fresh air, personal hygiene was also highly valued by reformers, and these values inspired some physical rebuilding of the North End.

The new Paul Revere School was completed in 1897 on Prince Street, near the corner of Salem Street. One controversial component of the school, according to the *Boston Globe*, was the proposed inclusion of showers

The Hancock School standing behind the buildings on Parmenter Street shortly after it was built. It was described at the time as costing thousands of dollars more than any other school in the city, and it was "not surpassed in any respect." The Hancock School remained a girls' school for most of the 1800s. *Private collection.*

The Thoreau House at 57 Prince Street, 1890s. As the sign proclaims, this house was built in 1727, and it was the home of John Thoreau, grandfather of Henry David Thoreau, from the early 1770s until 1800. The house remained in the Thoreau family until 1881. The proprietor, presumably Mr. L. Goldman, has dressed up for the photograph. The shop was demolished in 1896 to make way for the Revere School. *Courtesy of the Boston Public Library, Print Department.*

for the children. School committee members hotly debated the topic, and local experts weighed in with their opinions. The board of health chairman said that showers would "not only insure cleanliness in the school room, but [they] would give the children of the poor particularly an opportunity of bathing which they did not perhaps enjoy at home." He also argued that they would increase health and decrease the "dullness" felt by some children at school. One member of the school committee, Thomas Strange, objected because "it is all the teachers can do with the comparatively limited number of school days to give their children a proper education let alone having them washed." Mr. Strange recommended general public baths and was against bathing that was in any way the responsibility of school officials. In the end, the Paul Revere School was built with the new "bath rooms," and they were apparently successful because, by 1901, all the new schools in Boston included similar facilities.

Small-Scale Initiative

From the late 1840s through the 1880s, the North End was hopelessly overcrowded, filthy and, despite two centuries of ordinances to the contrary, still filled with wooden structures vulnerable to the devastation of fire. The neighborhood also housed a disproportionately large number of the city's poorest residents during that time, and they understandably had great difficulty investing in the physical improvement of the North End. Between the 1880s and about 1917, however, local residents had the means to slowly transform the district. During those four decades, North Enders demolished vast numbers of wooden structures and replaced them with the familiar four- and five-floor brick apartment buildings that still compose the dominant architectural style of the neighborhood. Although some of these buildings were overfilled, they were taller and more spacious than the structures that they replaced and, being built of brick, were more resistant to fire. The new buildings, combined with increased city services, improved living conditions in the North End. The city enhanced the new construction with more open space. The North End Park and Beach, Copp's Hill Terraces and the North End Playground were completed in 1896–1897. The beach served as a bathing facility for North Enders who lived in a neighborhood without adequate baths or regular plumbing. The North End now had one contiguous open space, from Hull Street across the cemetery and Charter Street, down the terraces and past Commercial Street all the way into the harbor.

The North End Beach, circa 1927. Separate bathhouses for men and women are in the background. The elevated tracks on Commercial Street can be seen at the far left. *Courtesy of the Boston Public Library, Print Department.*

Permanent Solutions

At the beginning of the twentieth century, the city invested heavily in upgrading public facilities in the North End, and much of that investment was made in the vicinity of North Bennet Street. The area around the North End Playground, between Tileston, Hanover, Parmenter and Salem Streets, was physically at the center of the North End. The Revere, Eliot and Ware Schools were located there, and the Christopher Columbus School was completed there in 1903, on the site of the Ware School. Five years later, the city opened a bathhouse on North Bennet Street, directly behind the Paul Revere School. In 1911, the city purchased St. John the Baptist Church, which was next to the Columbus School, and tore it down. A new Boston Public Library Branch was built on the site at a cost of $86,000.

By 1913, this central block of the North End contained a bathhouse, a library, two new public school buildings, a playground, a schoolyard and three older schools, including the Eliot, one of Boston's oldest educational

The North End Branch Library, built on North Bennet Street in 1912. Although there had been branch library locations in other buildings, this was the first branch for the neighborhood to have its own structure.

The Eliot School, circa 1865. This building was constructed shortly after the incident concerning young Thomas Whall. It is seen here from North Bennet Street, and it runs along the entire length of Wiggin Street to Tileston Street. This building was still fairly new when John F. Fitzgerald attended, and it remained in use until the early 1930s. There is currently a parking lot on the site. *Courtesy of the Bostonian Society/Old State House, Boston Streets Photograph Collection, circa 1865–1999.*

institutions. The Baptist Bethel and a branch of the United States Post Office sat at the Hanover Street end of North Bennet, while the Salem Street end housed the North Bennet Street Industrial School. St. Leonard's Catholic Church and an adjacent parochial school, St. Anthony's, and a friary were next to the playground. On April 6, 1913, the *Boston Globe* called North Bennet Street "Boston's Public Service Center." Although the North End remained overcrowded in the early twentieth century, services and improvements made by the city, as well as the erection of brick dwellings by residents and private investors, played a crucial part in the rehabilitation of the neighborhood.

The city planning board, led by the renowned architect Ralph Adams Cram, continually advocated for more improvements. Cram was a major force in Boston's early twentieth-century public improvement efforts. Unfortunately, when the city took over a parcel of land to create a playground or park, families already living in that area were usually displaced. Still, the physical changes made between 1895 and 1915 were relatively small, and the open spaces created were probably welcomed by the majority of residents. For example, Cram and the planning board created a park between Morton and Stillman Streets, which was completed by 1918. The small efforts frustrated the board, though, which thought that the North End was "still greatly in need of wholesale reformation if living conditions are to be made wholesome and agreeable." The term "wholesale reformation" meant the complete destruction of dozens of older buildings and small streets, with the concomitant removal

Webster Avenue, shown here in 1890, stretched from Hanover Street down to Unity Street, between Charter and Tileston. Several other smaller alleys emanated from Webster to the right and to the left. It was exactly the type of situation despised by the city planning board in the early 1900s. The city demolished the area between 1928 and 1933 to make way for the Paul Revere Mall, also known as "the Prado." *Courtesy of the Bostonian Society/Old State House, Boston Streets Photograph Collection, circa 1865–1999.*

of residents. Cram and his colleagues had become convinced that the crooked, tiny alleys of the North End had become "detrimental to the welfare of the city" and therefore they and their contents had to be destroyed. In the process, the board acknowledged that residents would probably be displaced, but it was "quite possible" that they would move to better quarters with the assistance of both public and private agencies.

The Folly of Lafayette Street

In 1919, the city planning board published a comprehensive plan for rebuilding a wholesome North End. It focused on the dwellings that had been built inside city blocks. These structures were often only accessed by tiny alleys or through tunnels underneath the buildings around them. If these dwellings were more than sixty feet away from an open space (such as a playground, a park or the cemetery), they needed to be removed. The plan identified dozens of locations throughout the neighborhood where it advocated the wholesale destruction of existing buildings. The 1919 plan even called for a "Paul Revere Park," which would have required the demolition of several buildings around the historic Paul Revere House, leaving the ancient building sitting alone amongst grass and trees.

The 1919 planners pointed out, quite rightly, that old wooden buildings in hard-to-access places were fire hazards. They also, however, viewed the buildings and the streets of the North End as a disease, as literally being dangerous to one's health. Even in the face of the latest health and social statistics, which revealed that the North End actually had *lower* rates of sickness, death, crime and delinquency than other parts of Boston, the planners were blinded by their concept of an "ideal" urban neighborhood. They explained away the positive statistics by arguing that many North Enders at the time were "from the sturdy races of Europe," and most of them were engaged in "hard but invigorating work," characteristics that gave them a certain resistance to the negative effects of the neighborhood's physical environment. However "sturdy" the Jewish and Italian residents were, the neighborhood would eventually, according to the planners, sicken them or their children.

The centerpiece of the 1919 plan was a new thoroughfare, from the Charlestown Bridge to Atlantic Avenue, near the Faneuil Hall market area. So as to avoid the difficult topography of Copp's Hill and the destruction of more valuable property closer to downtown, the new avenue, to be called Lafayette Street, would have swallowed part of Endicott Street, cut through

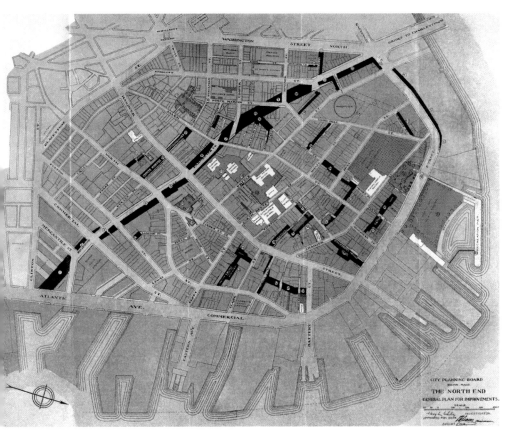

The North End General Plan for Improvements, published in 1919. The black areas, especially the long swath cut across the neighborhood, represent buildings and streets to be removed. Nearly all of the open space was eventually created, except for the park around Paul Revere's House. *Courtesy of the Boston Public Library, Print Department.*

the Jewish section of the neighborhood and engulfed Parmenter and Richmond Streets. Ultimately, this costly plan was never fully implemented, but several of its smaller recommendations were executed later.

Industrial Realities

Public utilities and private manufacturing companies increasingly industrialized the waterfront areas of the North End, while at the same time

Charter Street Park was built in 1971, and it resembles closely the city's 1919 plan
to create more open space in the congested blocks of the North End. The narrow
passageway that runs along the buildings at the left is Greenough Lane, which terminates
at Commercial Street.

the city expanded parks and playgrounds in the district, and the two processes
conflicted. For example, Boston Elevated Railway opened the new elevated
train between Charlestown and Roxbury in 1901. The elevated tracks traveled
down Commercial Street, separating the Copp's Hill Terraces from the North
End Park and Beach, before continuing down Atlantic Avenue and out of
the neighborhood. Another example was the gasworks that polluted the air
in the parks. The gasworks were on Commercial Street, between Prince and
Hull Streets, where they had been in one form or another since the 1820s.
The primary function of the gasworks was the storage and distribution of
illuminating gas for the city's streetlamps and private homes. Newspapers in
various cities from the late 1800s and early 1900s are filled with stories of
workers or neighbors being poisoned by leaking gas, policemen and firemen
being burned as they responded to explosions at various gasworks and the
constant fear of deadly accidents felt by people who lived near such facilities.
In 1896, North Enders complained to the city that the Boston Gas Light
Company was using inferior and unsafe materials at the gasworks. Local

State Street Station, at the intersection of State and Atlantic Avenue, circa 1911. This station was part of the elevated train system that ran through the North End. A similar station was located at Battery Street. *Courtesy of the Bostonian Society/Old State House, Gilbert Payson Lantern Slide Collection, circa 1905–1926.*

residents had brought this issue to the attention of the proper officials many times in the past, but the problem kept resurfacing.

People were afraid to go into their own basements because they worried that a lamp or candle might ignite leaking gas, and a suspiciously high number of people who lived near the gasworks on Prince Street were becoming sick. Unfortunately, the city ignored the protests and sold more land to the gas company. By 1895, the Boston Gas Light Company already owned everything between the Charles River and Charter, Snowhill and Prince Streets, except for a tiny triangle of housing along Hull, Snowhill and North Hudson Streets. By 1904, the company had expanded its facilities to the point that it erased some smaller lanes from the map. A couple of years later, it began construction on a huge new "gasometer," as the gas tanks were called, near the corner of Prince and Snowhill Streets. Although this was an affront to local residents, it also spoke to the large number of people using gaslights.

Purity Distilling Company, a subsidiary of the United States Industrial Alcohol Company, built another industrial menace on Commercial Street, not far from the gasometer, in 1915. It built a fifty-foot tank to hold over two million gallons of molasses. The sticky substance was in high demand at the time because it was necessary for the production of industrial alcohol, which was used in ammunition and explosives. Tragically, Purity poorly constructed the tank, and any North End schoolboy could tell you that it constantly leaked. On January 15, 1919, the tank ruptured, and a thirty-five-mile-per-hour wave of over two million gallons of molasses flooded Commercial Street. The flood killed 21 people, injured 150 more, mangled the elevated train tracks and destroyed several buildings. This event sparked new protests against dangerous industrial facilities that lacked safety precautions.

In light of this disaster, Joseph Langone, at that time a member of the Republican political organization called the Columbus Club, urged that the gasworks be removed from the North End. Local residents held a mass meeting at the North Bennet Street Industrial School on February 9,

The 1919 Molasses Flood mangled the elevated tracks on Commercial Street. *Courtesy of the Boston Public Library, Print Department.*

1919. Chaired by Vincent Brogna, the meeting included speeches by James Donnaruma, founder of the *Post-Gazette Newspaper* in the North End, and Ralph Adams Cram, who represented the city planning board. Those in attendance generally agreed that gasometers should be removed from all residential districts, and the group planned to petition the legislature to pass a bill establishing and enforcing a prohibition on the dangerous tanks. Although it took several more years of political agitation, the tank was finally dismantled. This victory was due to the increased political participation and power of Italian Americans, as well as the gas company's loss of business to the electric company.

The North End circa 1920. *Courtesy of the Boston Public Library, Print Department.*

The North End at Three Hundred

By the 1920s, the North End had come a long way from the days of the Black Sea, inadequate public facilities and a preponderance of overcrowded wooden houses. The neighborhood was still densely populated and ringed with industrial activities, but it was safer and more comfortable than it had been for decades. Many of the brick tenements and commercial buildings that were around at Boston's 300th birthday can still be seen across the neighborhood today. At the close of its third century, the North End was known as "Little Italy," but it still had a small remainder of a once large Jewish section.

CHAPTER 11

THE NORTH END'S JEWISH COLONY

etween the early 1880s, when the North Bennet Street Industrial School was firmly established, and about 1930, when the giant gasometer was dismantled, the Jewish community of the North End rose to its greatest height and then slowly diminished. There had been isolated Jewish residents from time to time in Boston since the 1600s, and the earliest Jewish Bostonians usually had Dutch, Spanish, Portuguese or Italian ancestry, rather than English. Because these individuals were spread out over so many decades, they lived and worked in the town without any Jewish neighbors and without the benefit of a synagogue or prayer community. Increase Mather had long been interested in the conversion of all Jews to Christianity, and he and his fellow Puritans pressured any Jews they met. Hebrew was a required subject at Harvard, but a full-time Hebrew instructor was not hired until 1723. That teacher was Judah Monis, Harvard's first instructor of Hebrew and a Jewish man of either Portuguese or Italian descent. Prior to his appointment, Monis wrote a complete guide to Hebrew grammar and was baptized a Christian at the college. It will never be known if Monis truly accepted Christianity, although Mather believed that he did, but it is certain that Monis felt a variety of pressures to renounce his Judaism.

In 1782, Moses Michael Hays and his family, the North End's first openly Jewish household, moved to Hanover Street. Originally from New York City, the Hayses had most recently lived in Newport, Rhode Island, before coming to Boston. Hays was a successful merchant in Newport, and he traded in watches, linens and food products. Newport already had an established Jewish community, complete with the Touro Synagogue, which survives today as the oldest Jewish temple in the United States. The synagogue was named for its first rabbi, Isaac Touro, who was Moses Hays's brother-in-law. British forces maintained control of Newport during the Revolution until late 1779, and Hays provided the Continental army with supplies as it attempted to liberate the town. After moving to the North End, Hays established an import/export business, engaged in some of the new trade with China and extended loans to other businessmen.

In 1784, Hays was one of the founders of the Bank of Massachusetts, a commercial bank that helped legitimize Boston as a financial center. Hays had been a Mason in New York and Newport, and he joined the Grand Lodge of Massachusetts in Boston, eventually becoming its grand master. Though he had always openly lived his life as a Jew, even before the Revolution, prior to his move he had the benefit of living in established Jewish communities in New York and Rhode Island. Once in Boston, the Hayses maintained their Judaism, though it must have been difficult to follow all Jewish customs without having a local Jewish cemetery, a "kosher" market or even a *minyan* (the required ten Jewish men to conduct prayer services). At least they were not pressured to convert, like Judah Monis, but the Jewish presence they created in the North End was fleeting. Beginning in the late 1830s, a large stream of Jewish immigrants from Central Europe came to America. Those who settled in Boston, however, avoided the North End, which at that time was in the process of becoming an Irish ghetto and a haven for gambling, drinking and prostitution.

A New Beginning

Starting in the 1870s, enough Jews lived in the North End to begin building elements of a stable Jewish community. Besides a minyan, a Jewish community also needed several other components in order to successfully practice the Jewish way of life. A handful of *chevras* ("societies" or "associations") sprung up in the Hanover Street area. The chevra was responsible for arranging for the most basic needs, such as renting a hall for prayers, preparing bodies for burial in case of death, acquiring appropriate burial land and facilitating access to kosher meats by hiring a *schochet* (kosher "butcher"). A chevra also provided charitable services among the Jewish population. As the number of Jews in the North End increased, they added other services, including Hebrew schools, religious paraphernalia stores and *matza* factories, and, once all of these needs were met, constructed synagogues. These buildings signaled the intention of the Jewish people in the North End to put down deeper roots, and the synagogue became not only the religious meeting place of the community but also the educational, charitable, political and social center.

The Wells House at 115–125 Salem Street, as seen from Cooper Street, just before its demolition in 1895. H. Wiess Boots and Shoes is located on the ground floor. The Hancock School is rising behind it. *Courtesy of the Bostonian Society/Old State House, Boston Streets Photograph Collection, circa 1865–1999.*

In the early 1870s, a group calling itself Shomre Shabbos ("observers of the Sabbath") rented space on Elm Street, near Hanover Street, in what is now Government Center Plaza. It organized prayer services for the Russian-Polish Jewish immigrants, and it wasn't long before it acquired a burial ground in Dedham, a town on the western border of Boston. Shomre Shabbos eventually settled on Hanover Street, at the corner of Fleet Street. In 1875, another group, called Shomre Beth Abraham, catering to Lithuanian Jewish immigrants, rented worship space on Hanover Street in Cockerel Hall. Millions of Jewish people emigrated from Europe during the last two decades of the nineteenth century, and Boston absorbed about ninety thousand of them between 1880 and the beginning of the First World War. As more Jewish people moved into the North End, they settled in the area along Salem Street, between Wiget and Noyes, and then spread farther along Salem Street and beyond Prince and North Margin Streets. There were slightly more Italians than Jews in the North End by 1895, but both groups together outnumbered the Irish population, which was still concentrated around St. Stephen's and St. Mary's.

Salem Street, circa 1893, across from Cooper Street. In the foreground is a Jewish peddler, and in the background is the Wells House. The Wells House was built in the 1670s, not long before Paul Revere's House was constructed. North End legend says that the first group of Baptists in Boston secretly met in this building until they built their nearby church in 1679. *Courtesy of the Boston Public Library, Print Department.*

North End Temples

By the 1880s, Boston had attracted a rabbi, Moses Margolis, who had been educated at Bialystok, in Poland. He had served as a rabbi in various locations in Eastern Europe for thirteen years before coming to Boston. He found small Jewish organizations, like Shomre Shabbos, in the North and West Ends and united several of the smaller groups. One congregation, Shomre Beth Abraham, had grown large enough to thrive without being combined with any other group. In fact, some of the younger members of Shomre Beth Abraham decided to leave Cockerel Hall and form a new worship community called Beth Israel. In 1888, Congregation Beth Israel purchased the Home for Little Wanderers on Baldwin Place, which had been constructed in 1810 as the Second Baptist Church. Beth Israel, usually called the "Baldwin Place Shul," was dedicated in 1890, with Margolis serving as rabbi.

Recognized as the chief rabbi of Boston, Rabbi Margolis stayed with Beth Israel in the North End until 1905. As the Protestant church congregations and prominent individual Christians established missions and services throughout the North End, Margolis helped the Jewish community organize

Beth Israel's sanctuary, early 1900s. *Donated anonymously to the Vilna Shul in memory of Leah Bachcofsky, who came to Boston from Vilna in the 1900s.*

its own social programs. For example, it opened a home for elderly and infirm Jewish people, called the B'Noth Israel Sheltering Home, on Cooper Street. Beth Israel almost immediately created a Hebrew School on Baldwin Place after the dedication of its synagogue. Margolis also organized a burial society, a loan office and a home for poor Jewish children called Helping Hand. Margolis's leadership skills were so impressive that Jewish groups in New York tried to lure him from Boston. Eventually, Margolis did leave town to become the rabbi of Congregation Kehilath Jeshurun on East Eighty-fifth Street in New York City. More than two thousand people gathered to see him off on December 27, 1905. One reason he gave for his move to New York was that his only daughter lived there, and he wished to be closer to her. It is not surprising that Rabbi Margolis became a great leader of New York's Jewish community, where he was known as "the RaMaZ." Congregation Kehilath Jeshurun is still a thriving synagogue in New York and is still affiliated with the nearby Ramaz School.

Shaarei Yerushalayim, another North End Jewish congregation, was founded in 1889. It worshiped at 13 Salem Street, an area now covered by the new "Greenway" parks. Under the leadership of its rabbi, Solomon Friederman,

Prince Hall Masons gathered to honor their founder on Copp's Hill in the early 1900s. Events such as these reminded Jewish and Italian North Enders of the long and complex history of their neighborhood. *Courtesy of the Museum of African American History, Boston, Massachusetts.*

in 1903, the congregation constructed the only new synagogue ever built in the North End, located in an alley called Carroll Place, adjacent to Baldwin Place. Shaarei Yerushalayim's new building was very close to Beth Israel on Baldwin Place and therefore at the physical center of the North End Jewish community. The construction of the synagogue was significant because, in the early twentieth century, new Jewish synagogues, as opposed to converted church buildings or rented halls, were primarily built in the West End, Roxbury and Chelsea. In honor of this milestone in North End history, as well as the Jewish community's commitment to the neighborhood, Carroll Place was officially renamed Jerusalem Place upon the 1903 dedication of the Shaarei Yerushalayim Synagogue (Shaarei Yerushalayim means "Gates of Jerusalem").

Rabbi Friederman was also a very active and successful force in the Jewish community of the North End and beyond. He was invited to participate at the dedication of new synagogues and at fundraising events to assist existing congregations in Roxbury, Chelsea and East Boston. In the early twentieth century, these were all areas in which Jewish people moving up and out of the North and West Ends began to settle. In 1903, the *Boston Globe* considered

This Jerusalem Place arch with the faded words "Hebrew School" is a reminder of Congregation Shaarei Yerushalayim.

Friederman to be a "Representative Hebrew of Boston." Years later, in 1909, he successfully negotiated with the city's school board to ensure that a drill at the English High School in May would end before sunset, so that the Jewish students could return home in time for the beginning of the Sabbath. Friederman and his congregation on Jerusalem Place also helped create the Hebrew Immigrant Aid Society, a Hebrew School for children, a *Talmud* (a collection of centuries of Jewish scholarship) study group, a Home for Aged Orthodox Hebrews in Watertown and a Rabbinical school. Some members of his congregation may also have been involved in the protests to remove the gasometer from the neighborhood because illuminating gas had caused an explosion at Shaarei Yerushalayim in the summer of 1905—the accident thankfully did not kill or seriously injure anyone.

The Community Relocates

Friederman stayed in the North End until 1922, when he left to become the rabbi of a congregation in Roxbury. By then, there were very few Jewish people left in the neighborhood, which was becoming increasingly Italian. Beth Israel had attracted another rabbi, Wolf Margolis, after a lengthy search. Unfortunately, he too left for New York, after only four years in the North End. Members of Beth Israel, especially younger members, increasingly moved to places like Roxbury, where former North Enders and others built a thriving Jewish community. The city purchased Beth Israel's synagogue on Baldwin Place in April 1922 and demolished it with the intention of building a playground and open space for the North End. Beth Israel's hand-carved ark, the holy space in the sanctuary where the Torah scrolls are kept, was saved and installed in Temple B'nai Brith in Somerville upon the completion of their building in 1922. It is still in use today.

Boston's first George Robert White Fund Health Unit was opened on North Margin Street in 1924 on the site of Beth Israel Synagogue. Today, it is home to the Knights of Columbus. *Courtesy of the Boston Public Library, Print Department.*

George Robert White, a wealthy Boston businessman and philanthropist, passed away in 1922. Among other gifts to Boston institutions, he left a fund to create works of public utility and beauty throughout the city. In 1924, the city constructed and opened the first neighborhood health center utilizing the White Fund. The new center was built on the former site of Beth Israel, fronting on North Margin Street. Although many older North Enders of

Jerusalem Place, 1943. This may be a view of the northern side of the vacant Shaarei Yerushalayim Synagogue, taken just before it was demolished. Despite being the first and only building deliberately constructed as a synagogue in the North End, I have yet to find a confirmed image of the building. *Courtesy of Historic New England.*

today remember going to the center for medical attention, especially dental work, this same building has been home to the local Knights of Columbus since the 1960s. With the destruction of the North End's main synagogue in 1922 and the departure of Friederman, the Jewish presence in the district was coming to an end. Shaarei Yerushalayim's temple was abandoned during the Great Depression of the 1930s and was finally demolished at the end of World War II.

Many Jewish shop owners retained their businesses, especially clothing and dry goods stores on Salem Street, even after they had moved out of the neighborhood. Older North Enders today easily recall shopping in Jewish-owned local stores in their youth. Unfortunately, today there are no traces of the North End Union's Jewish comedy troupe, the synagogues off of Salem Street or any kosher shops. The most tangible reminder of the Jews of the North End is the street sign at Jerusalem Place.

CHAPTER 12

LITTLE ITALY

During the early 1880s, there were still many more Irish people in the North End than all of the Italian, Portuguese and Jewish people combined. By 1890, however, parts of the North End near North Square were known as Boston's "Little Italy." In another two decades, the name was properly applied to the majority of the neighborhood. The history of Italians in the North End has been well chronicled in recent years. In addition, that same history still lives in the memories of thousands of native North Enders. The focus of this chapter, then, will be the contours of life in Little Italy from the 1880s through the 1970s, rather than Italian-American history in particular.

Sacred Heart

In the nineteenth century, Italians were not yet in control of neighborhood affairs, a fact that was especially true in the Catholic churches. Despite the relatively new St. Mary's and the enlarged St. Stephen's, enough Irish people were attending St. Leonard's to make a portion of the Italian congregation feel as though it was losing control of its church. In 1884, a group of Italian people formed the San Marco Society and purchased Father Taylor's bethel in North Square. After making some alterations, the San Marco Society asked the Boston Archdiocese to dedicate the church and supply a priest. Archbishop John Joseph Williams was, to say the least, not happy with this independent group of Catholics and refused to recognize the new church until the property was turned over to the archdiocese. Williams and the San Marco Society disputed the issue for nearly five years. In the end, the society agreed to relinquish its property, and the building was dedicated as the Church of the Sacred Heart, an Italian national church. According to the deed, however, the land had to be used for worship and for the benefit of the Italian Roman Catholics of Boston. Those stipulations became very important in saving Sacred Heart from closure during the scandals and financial difficulties that would come more than a century later.

"Michael Angelo"

By 1910, Italians and Italian Americans were quickly spreading across the remaining Irish-American sections of the neighborhood and squeezing the Jewish enclave. In 1917, when the United States became involved in the First World War, a wave of xenophobia washed over the country. Some of the many immigrants in America were born in enemy nations, and all immigrants were viewed as possible spies. The *Boston Globe* reported on a scare in May 1916, which was based on false rumors. Many North Enders believed that a German was "jabbing poisonous needles" into children at the Cushman and Hancock Schools and "injecting German blood into hitherto unsullied Italian veins." Dozens of parents showed up and demanded to see their children immediately. In another example of anti-foreign sentiment, one month after the United States joined the war, the Boston School Committee threatened its European employees: become citizens or be fired. During the same time, however, the committee did make a positive gesture toward the Italian community.

In honor of the U.S. alliance with Italy in the war, a new school built in the North End was given an Italian name. The building was constructed on Charter Street, between the cemetery and Phipps Place, which was named in honor of Governor William Phips's seventeenth-century estate. The naming of the building, though, showed a lack of understanding of Italian language and culture on the part of the school committee. The school was dubbed "Michael Angelo," and Phipps Place was renamed Angelo Street. At a school committee meeting a few years later, "a request was introduced [that was] signed by Italian citizens of the North End" to correct the spelling of the Michael Angelo School. The committee agreed that it was "desirable" to change it to the "Michelangelo School" so as to be "in conformity with the best usage." The name of the school was changed, and in April 1923, Angelo Street became Michelangelo Street. To this day, it is the only street in Little Italy with an Italian name.

Business

Atlantic Avenue and Commercial Street were filled with commercial enterprises that employed North Enders from the nineteenth century through the 1950s. Union Freight Company tracks were embedded all along these two major roads, detouring into the Quincy Market Cold Storage property and the Mercantile and Clinton Street Markets. Ships and wagons, followed by trains and then trucks, transported, stored, distributed and sold produce and fish along the waterfront. Quincy Market Cold Storage occupied the area that is now the Christopher Columbus Plaza apartment building between the Commercial Wharf buildings and Richmond Street. Below Richmond Street was the Mercantile Market down to Clinton Street, with the adjacent Clinton Market and the Faneuil Hall Market. Factories producing chocolate, candy, pasta, shoes and textiles ringed the North End, as did canneries and bottling plants, as well as metalworking, masonry and import/export companies. The North End fishing fleet employed many locals, either as fishermen or as employees in the fish markets or canneries. From the late 1800s through the 1920s, butchers, both kosher and not; matza and *maccheroni* factories; peddlers' carts filled with fruit; bakeries making bread and pizza; shops with imported foods; and stores with religious and devotional items were crowded along most of the North End's streets.

Bakeries and little restaurants opened throughout the neighborhood to serve the local population, in addition to small shops and groceries. Parziale's Bakery at 80 Prince Street is one of the few survivors from the early years of Little Italy. The Pastene Company, now a national brand, was founded even earlier and operated on Fulton Street. Through his store, Pietro Pastene supplied the neighborhood with imported Italian goods. The Prince line of pasta, also a national brand today, was in operation prior to World War I, and it took its name from the street where it was founded, a few doors down from Parziale's, at number 92. The Prince factory later expanded and moved to the waterfront, and the old building, now condominiums, still stands at 63 Atlantic Avenue. Many people will remember the "Wednesday is Prince Spaghetti Day" ads. The 1969 television commercial showed young Anthony Martignetti hearing his mother calling him and running home for a spaghetti dinner. Of course, anyone familiar with the neighborhood could see that Anthony was running through the Haymarket area on Blackstone Street, and he could not possibly have heard his mother calling no matter where she was in the neighborhood, which was on the other side of the elevated highway.

Education

The Eliot School is the oldest educational institution in the North End. Its roots can be traced back to the original North Writing School founded on Tileston Street in 1700. Students at the North Writing School were given a practical education, centered on arithmetic, reading and, of course, writing and penmanship. Prior to attendance at any of the writing schools in Boston, many children may have already learned to read, either at home or at a "Dame School," privately funded nurseries that taught reading skills. Very young boys and girls attended Dame Schools, which were usually run in the home of the teacher. This practical education, combined with spiritual instruction at home and at church, was expanded in the writing schools. For a classical education after the writing school, a young man would attend one of the Latin schools in Boston. The North Grammar School, the Latin school in the North End, was founded on Tileston Street in 1713. At a Latin school, a student could learn the ancient language, as well as some philosophy and history derived from the ancient Greeks and Hebrews.

After the Revolution, the North Grammar School was discontinued by the selectmen, and the North Writing School expanded into its Tileston Street building. The city constructed a new building in 1931, on the site of Paul Revere's last home on Charter Street, where the school remains to this day. Between 1903 and World War II, the North End was also home to the Michelangelo, Christopher Columbus, Paul Revere, Charlotte Cushman and John Hancock public schools. During the same time, the neighborhood also benefited from the local Catholic schools, namely St. John's on Moon Street, St. Mary's on Cooper Street and St. Anthony's on North Bennet Street. The North Bennet Street Industrial School was another available choice. There was notably no high school in the North End during those years, so teenagers had to attend high schools in places like Brighton, Charlestown or Roxbury.

The city closed the Columbus Grammar School in 1943, and the building was used as a military facility for the remainder of World War II, complete with a prison for POWs, including Italians. The Catholic Archdiocese purchased the building and reopened it as a high school after the war ended. Part of the building was the Columbus High School for boys, and the other part of the building was the Julie Billiart High School for girls. Over the next decade, the Catholic Archdiocese of Boston also purchased the Cushman, Hancock and Revere Schools. The Revere School was converted into St. Anthony's School, which had been operating for years in a smaller building. The Cushman and the Hancock Schools were demolished to make way for a gymnasium, known to locals as the "C.C. Center." By the 1950s, then, the only remaining public schools in the North End were the Eliot and the Michelangelo Schools. However, a parochial education was now available from elementary through high school.

Transportation

After the First World War, city planners and transportation officials sought new ways to connect Boston to the people who had moved far to the north, west and south of the city but still worked or owned property in Boston. In 1929, the state authorized the construction of a vehicular tunnel between East Boston and Boston's North End. By then, the neighborhoods on either side of the tunnel were distinctly Italian in heritage. Boston Airport, known today as Logan International Airport, had been dedicated in East Boston in 1923, and the proposed tunnel was needed to connect Boston to both the commuters north of the city and to the important commercial cargo flying into the airport. The tunnel was completed in 1934, traveling from East Boston under the harbor and entering the North End under Lincoln's Wharf. It continues underneath North Square and emerges near Cross Street, between Hanover and North Streets. The buildings between Board Alley and Hanover, Cross and North Streets were destroyed during the tunnel project, except for those that fronted on Hanover Street. Board Alley and Mechanic Street were severed to accommodate the entrance of the tunnel.

A new tunnel administration building was completed in 1932 along North Street, on the other side of the tunnel opening, to house offices and equipment necessary to operate the new tunnel. This harbor tunnel was named for someone associated with the East Boston side—William Hyslop Sumner, who was born into a wealthy and influential family in Roxbury in 1780. He served in the War of 1812 and was later elected to the Massachusetts legislature. Sumner is perhaps best known for his physical and commercial development of East Boston and for his account of history in that neighborhood, published in 1858. As the Sumner Tunnel opened, ridership on the elevated train had declined so much that the tracks along Commercial Street and Atlantic Avenue, along with the passenger station at Battery Street, were closed. During the Second World War, the North End tracks were completely dismantled and used for scrap metal.

After the war, an influx of federal funds accelerated the growth of the suburbs by paying for the construction of a network of high-speed,

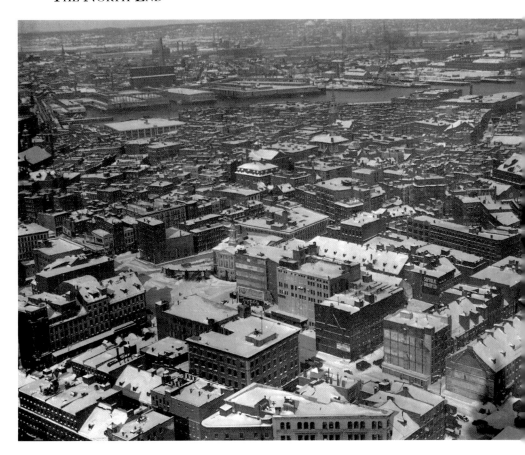

The North End, circa 1934. *Courtesy of the Boston Public Library, Print Department.*

multilane roads. One of these roads was built in the early 1950s through downtown Boston, to connect the communities to the north and south. The highway was authorized in 1949, and hundreds of North End buildings were destroyed below Cross Street, from the Charles River all the way beyond Atlantic Avenue. Named for the influential North Ender who had passed away in the fall of 1950, the "John F. Fitzgerald Expressway" opened through the North End in 1954. This elevated highway, with its series of on- and offramps, severed the North End from the rest of the city by truncating North Washington, Endicott, Salem, Hanover, North, Fulton and Commercial Streets. The increased traffic created the opportunity for the state to authorize a second tunnel between the North End and East Boston.

The North End stands behind the elevated "Central Artery" at the right of this early 1960s photo. The state demolished the Central Artery and built an underground highway along the same route. *Courtesy of the Bostonian Society/Old State House, Robert B. Severy Photograph Collection, circa 1962–1963.*

North Shore commuters and Logan Airport passengers required more capacity than the Sumner Tunnel could offer. The new tunnel, which opened in 1961, was built parallel to the Sumner, entering the North End under Union Wharf. It passes to the south of North Square and emerges just before Richmond Street, between North and Fulton. Buildings were destroyed near the opening of the tunnel just before Richmond Street, and most of the buildings and streets between Richmond, Fulton, Cross and North were also removed. Ferry Street, the birthplace of John F. Fitzgerald, and the surrounding small streets and alleys were wiped away to create the tunnel entrance. The tunnel was named after Lieutenant William F. Callahan Jr., whose father was the chairman of the Massachusetts Turnpike Authority. In 1945, Lieutenant Callahan had been killed in service to the United States in Italy.

A Safe Place

The construction of the expressway took a huge toll on the people of the North End. Many people lost their homes and livelihoods, and thousands

John F. Fitzgerald (1863–1950) of Hanover Street, 1910. As a city councilor in the 1890s, he secured authorization and funding to build the North End Park. In 1905, he became the first American-born person of Irish descent elected mayor of Boston. Fitzgerald also served in the Massachusetts legislature and the U.S. Congress. *Courtesy of the Boston Public Library, Print Department.*

of adjacent residents had to live with years of dust, noise and disorder. This large project also decreased the population of the neighborhood and thereby interrupted a slow process of physical rehabilitation that had been underway for decades. Still, after the highway opened in 1954, North Enders continued to use small amounts of money and the trade skills of various residents to rehabilitate building after building in the neighborhood. In this way, they built on the earlier investments by property owners and the city that had begun in the late nineteenth century. By the 1950s, the neighborhood had extremely low disease and mortality rates and very little street crime, just as it had back in the 1920s. Shops and residences, industry and recreation, services and entertainment comingled in the multiuse buildings and blocks. In 1959, the city planning writer, Jane Jacobs, described the North End's streets as "probably as safe as any place on Earth" in her book *The Death and Life of Great American Cities*. In stark contrast to the ideas of earlier planners like Ralph Adams Cram, Jacobs believed that the very streets of the North End helped to keep the neighborhood safe because of the small, manageable blocks, the constant foot traffic and the watchful eyes of shopkeepers and residents.

In addition to the destruction caused by the expressway, authorities had also developed a scheme for "massive clearance around historic buildings" that would have destroyed entire streets around places like the Old North Church. Jacobs derisively characterized city officials as "ashamed that at present tourists and school children may be distracted by the irrelevant North End while taking in the meaning of American freedom." Fortunately, this particular plan never came to fruition. The positive description of the North End in Jacobs's prominent book helped, in part, to save the North End from further mega-projects and other forms of "urban renewal." The work of Italian-American politicians in the 1960s, combined with the revulsion felt because of the wholesale destruction of the adjacent West End between 1958 and 1960, was also instrumental in stopping urban planners who saw a slum rather than a vibrant, working-class neighborhood. Unfortunately, planners and government officials had more ideas for redevelopment in the North End, and the Italian-American neighborhood would have to fight for its survival throughout the 1960s and 1970s.

Desegregation and Population Loss

North Enders in the 1960s and 1970s were living during a time when the United States was grappling with the internal effects of its own history. In the summer of 1963, about 200,000 people marched on Washington for equal civil rights. Closer to home, Boston's public school system still maintained separate white and black schools, even though racially segregated schools were nationally outlawed in 1954. The Boston School Committee continually ignored directives from the state to desegregate its schools, and the African-American community continued its efforts to change the system. Finally, in 1972, black Bostonians, along with a wide coalition of allies, sued the Boston School Committee in federal court on the grounds that the city deliberately maintained a segregated school system in which more resources were channeled to the predominantly white schools. The federal judge in the case concurred—to desegregate the schools and improve the quality of education, he ordered the city to transport black students to white schools, and vice versa. Because the North End had only one public elementary school, one public middle school and no public high school, young people of the North End who did not attend Catholic schools were affected by the plan.

Black parents had been working for two decades to end discrimination against their children in the public schools, and it is doubtful that they believed South Boston High School, where some of their children were sent, was any better than their local Dorchester High School. On the other hand, white parents felt that the federal government had no business intruding on local affairs and did not want their children transported to poor-quality schools in other neighborhoods. Racially charged tension and violence erupted throughout the city. Families who could afford to relocate left Boston. North End shops continued to close, especially along the once bustling Salem Street, and the waterfront industries dispersed or disappeared. The North End fishing fleet was all but gone by 1975, and the surviving wholesale fish markets moved to Fish Pier, farther down the Boston waterfront. The produce wholesalers moved to Chelsea, and the meat markets moved to the South Bay section of Roxbury.

A Presidential Visit

Resistance to the civil rights movement also produced assassinations of prominent men and the murders of young reformers. The same period was also marred by the wars in Indochina and the Watergate political scandal in Washington. Amidst all of the turmoil, transition and violence, President Gerald Ford paid a visit to the North End. On April 18, 1975, Ford traveled to the Old North Church to light a ceremonial "third lantern" on the 200th anniversary of the lighting of the original two signal lanterns on the eve of the Revolution. The president also took the opportunity to remark on how the United States had survived many challenges during its first two centuries. Referring to the turbulent times during which he became president, he said, "There are few times in our history when the American people have spoken with more eloquent reason and hope than during the tribulations and tests that our Government and our economic system have endured during the past year." He also said that "the two lanterns of Old North Church have fired a torch of freedom that has been carried to the ends of the world," and he asked the gathered crowd to pray with him that the United States would continue to be "a society which combined reason with liberty and hope with freedom." After his remarks, Ford lit the third lantern to inaugurate America's third century. The third lantern still hangs in the church today.

President Gerald Ford (1913–2006) at the Old North Church on April 18, 1975. *Courtesy of the Massachusetts Historical Society and the Old North Foundation Archives.*

The Bicentennial

On April 19, President Ford visited Concord and Lexington to join the Patriots Day ceremonies in both towns. His speeches in those locations, like that in the North End, talked about fulfilling the American dream together, as a unified people. He spoke of healing divisions rather than assigning blame. Kevin White, who had been mayor of Boston since 1968, was inspired by America's Bicentennial and Ford's vision of it as a time for reconciliation. In 1976, White threw a huge Bicentennial party, which began on July 4 with a concert by the Boston Symphony Esplanade Orchestra. The next big event came on July 10, with the arrival of the Tall Ships, which were escorted by the oldest surviving vessel built in the North End, the USS *Constitution*. The ship was built and launched in 1797, and it is the world's oldest commissioned vessel still afloat. The *Constitution* went out to sea and fired its cannons for the first time in one hundred years as it escorted the visiting Tall Ships from Poland, Portugal, Norway and Spain, as well as over sixty smaller craft from various countries, in 1976. The celebration continued the following day

Boston 200™

The Official Visit
of
Her Majesty Queen Elizabeth II
and
His Royal Highness
The Prince Philip, Duke of Edinburgh
to
Boston, Massachusetts
Sunday, July 11, 1976

PROGRAM

9:20 AM — U.S.S. *Constitution* fires twenty-one gun National Salute to Royal party aboard *HMY Britannia* as *Britannia* enters Boston Harbor between Castle and Deer Islands.

10:30 AM — Royal party disembarks *HMY Britannia* at Boston Coast Guard Base.
Music: United States Coast Guard Band

10:45 A.M. — Royal party arrives at the Old North Church (Christ Church) for Sunday morning worship.

11:40 AM — After the morning worship, Her Majesty receives replica of a Paul Revere chalice from Dr. Rev. Robert W. Golledge, vicar of the Old North Church, and a small bouquet of flowers from eleven-year-old Andrea Casali.

11:43 AM — Royal party departs Church for walk through Paul Revere Mall (The Prado).
Music: Cambridge Citadel Silver Band (Salvation Army).

12 noon — Royal party attends commemorative ceremony at Old State House, arriving via State Street through an honor cordon of OPERATION SAIL '76 cadets.
Ceremony: Welcoming Remarks
The Honorable Kevin H. White
Mayor of Boston
Sestina for The Queen
Mr. David McCord
Historical Address
Mr. Walter Muir Whitehill
Brief Reply
Her Majesty Queen Elizabeth II
Music: Royal Marines Band (from *HMY Britannia*)
Handel and Haydn Society (performing work by Conrad Susa specially composed for the occasion).

12:30 PM — Royal party departs Old State House for walk to City Hall. The route through Washington Mall is lined on both sides with an honor cordon of Revolutionary era militia troops from throughout New England.
Music: United States Army Band of New England
Empire Brass Quintet (performing selections from *The American Brass Band Journal*).

12:40 PM — Royal party attends reception and luncheon given by The Honorable Kevin H. White (inside City Hall).

12:55-2:35 PM — Public entertainment in City Hall Plaza.
Stage 1: Ronald Ingraham Concert Choir (performing American gospel music)
Stage 2: Mandala Dancers (performing American dances)
Stage 3: Members of the Country Song and Dance Society (performing early American music)

2:40 PM — Royal party departs City Hall for walk to Samuel Adams Park. Their route is lined on both sides with an honor cordon of Revolutionary era militia troops from throughout New England.
Music: Empire Brass Quintet (performing works from *The American Brass Band Journal*).

2:55 PM — Royal party reviews parade of Revolutionary era militia troops, lead by the Royal Marines Band (from *HMY Britannia*) and the Ancient and Honorable Artillery Company.

3:15 PM — Her Majesty receives a sterling teaspoon set given to her by the Ancient and Honorable Artillery Company.

3:20 PM — Royal party and motorcade tours Boston's Beacon Hill and Back Bay sections enroute to *U.S.S. Constitution* via Memorial Drive.

3:50 PM — Royal party tours *U.S.S. Constitution*.
Music: United States Navy Band (northeast region)

4:10 PM — Royal party boards *HMY Britannia*, Pier 1 west, Constitution Park.

7:30 PM — *HMY Britannia* sails for Canada.

The program for the royal visit to Boston in 1976 for the Bicentennial. The North End was the first stop for the British visitors. *Courtesy of Emily Piccolo*.

when the first reigning British monarch to ever visit Boston arrived in the North End. Queen Elizabeth II and her husband, Prince Philip, pulled into Boston Harbor aboard the HMY *Britannia*. They were greeted by a twenty-one-gun salute from the *Constitution*.

The royal party disembarked at the U.S. Coast Guard base at the end of Hanover Street and made its way to the Old North Church for Sunday morning services. When Old North was founded in 1723, it was an Anglican—or Church of England—house of worship. After the Revolution, Anglican churches in the United States were reorganized as the Episcopal Church, so the royal visitors found the services to be familiar. The rebuilding campaign after the 1954 hurricane, as well as the success of tourism in Boston over the following two decades, not only helped to preserve the Old North Church but also assured the church's spot on the short list of historic stops chosen for the brief royal visit to the city. After the worship services, the royal party visited the Old State House and the *Constitution*. According to

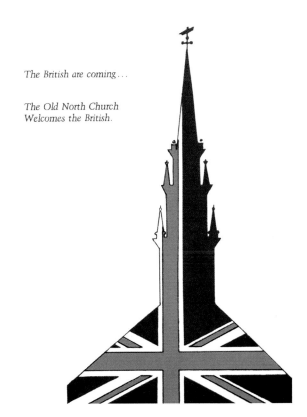

The British are coming . . .

The Old North Church
Welcomes the British.

The program for the Sunday morning services attended by Queen Elizabeth II and Prince Philip, on July 11, 1976, at the Old North Church. The cover shows the outline of the church filled with the British colors and utilizes the popular but historically inaccurate phrase. *Courtesy of Emily Piccolo.*

the *Boston Globe*, the queen told the crowd assembled at the Old State House, "One of the many good things about the Bicentennial celebrations is that they have encouraged us all to brush up our history." She went on to say:

> *We have enjoyed tremendously joining with the people of America in the celebrations of the Bicentenary...At the Old North Church last year, your President lit a third lantern dedicated to America's third century of freedom and to renewed faith in the American ideals. May its light never be dimmed.*

Queen Elizabeth II and Reverend Robert W. Golledge (1933–2005) at the Old North Church after services on Sunday, July 11, 1976. *Courtesy of the Massachusetts Historical Society and the Old North Foundation Archives.*

(Re-)Gentrification

In the summer of 1964, St. Stephen's Catholic Church on Hanover Street temporarily closed. Cardinal Richard Cushing, the Catholic archbishop of Boston, had decided to restore the historic edifice to its original appearance. St. Stephen's was designed by Charles Bulfinch, and it is the last of his churches still standing in Boston. Dedicated in 1804 as the second home of New North, the building became a Catholic church in 1862. The interior was extensively altered and embellished, and the entire building was raised over six feet in 1870 to accommodate a basement-level worship and activity space. By 1965, after a year of extensive work, St. Stephen's was lowered to its original height, and lighting fixtures, stairways, window and door openings and all other interior and exterior details were restored to Bulfinch's design. After the restoration, St. Stephen's reopened as a Catholic church and as a popular stop for tourists. The *Pilot*, Boston's official Catholic newspaper, called the work "simply the most extensive job of restoration ever undertaken by the Archdiocese of Boston."

Cardinal Cushing's decision to close and restore St. Stephen's was a sign of change. The population of the neighborhood was dwindling, and fewer churches and schools were needed. North Enders continued to move to the

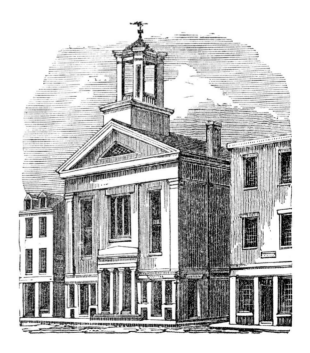

The First Universalist Church on Hanover Street, at the corner of North Bennet. This structure was built in 1838 as the second home for this congregation, whose original minister was John Murray, the founder of Universalism in America. The congregation vacated the building in 1864, and it was subsequently home to the Baptist Bethel. In the early 1970s, the building was converted for use as the North End Community Health Center.

suburbs, just as the descendants of Italian, Irish and Jewish immigrants were doing across the city and the nation. In 1973, the archdiocese closed St. Mary's school, Boston's first Catholic school, dating back to the 1840s. St. Mary's Catholic Church, the first in the North End, was closed and demolished a few years later. The Baptist Bethel, located in the 1838 Universalist Church at 332 Hanover Street, closed in 1972 and was soon reopened as the North End Community Health Center. The bathhouse on North Bennet Street was converted in the 1970s into a community center. Even as late as 1940, about 90 percent of North End homes were without private baths and about 50 percent lacked private toilets. Thirty years later, however, North Enders had renovated their homes by updating the plumbing and electrical wiring and combining smaller units into larger apartments.

The Boston Redevelopment Authority (BRA) continued to push renewal plans in the North End during the 1960s and 1970s. The Prince factory and the Lewis Wharf buildings on Atlantic Avenue were successfully recycled into housing, but the BRA mainly sought out and approved high-rise, high-density

The North End Community Health Center at 332 Hanover Street. This building has retained many of its original features, including most of the pediment, part of the cupola and the layout of the windows.

The Nazzaro Community Center on North Bennet Street was erected in 1908 as the North End Bathhouse, and it was converted into a community center in the 1970s. Part of the Revere School building is visible at the left.

projects, including the Charles River Park buildings (1962) on the former West End; the Prudential (1965) and the Hancock (1976) in the Back Bay; and the Kennedy Federal Building (1967) in the new Government Center. In fact, the BRA intended to take all of the land between the Callahan Tunnel and Atlantic Avenue, north of Cross Street, for the construction of similar towers with luxury residences and spectacular views. The Harbor Towers were completed on the waterfront near the North End in 1971. This activity prompted City Councilor Fred Langone to lead a coalition of North End residents and elected officials to block the construction of additional housing that North Enders, especially the elderly, could not afford. Fred Langone was a third-generation North End politician and the grandson of Joseph Langone, who had fought against the gasometer fifty years earlier.

Langone and others were largely successful. Between 1975 and 1980, they utilized federal subsidies to build housing for the elderly and the infirm, including Christopher Columbus Plaza over the old Union Freight Yard and Quincy Market Cold Storage; Ausonia Apartments on Fulton Street; and Casa Maria Apartments on the former site of St. Mary's Church (complete

Casa Maria Apartments on Endicott Street, on the former site of St. Mary's Church. The size of the building implies the grand scale of the second St. Mary's Church (1877–1979).

with a St. Mary's Chapel occupying part of the first floor). In addition, Atlantic Avenue was partially rerouted to create the Waterfront Park in 1976, known today as Christopher Columbus Park. Some nineteenth-century commercial structures on Fulton Street were destroyed to build the Ausonia Apartments, but dozens of other buildings along Fulton Street were saved and rehabilitated into housing, as were the Commercial and Mercantile blocks. Finally, the North End Nursing Home opened in 1983 at Fulton and Richmond Streets, thereby completing ten years of construction and renovation designed to keep the North End affordable for older Italian Americans. The trend continued when St. Anthony's School, located in the old Paul Revere School building, closed in 1982. It was reopened as mixed-income housing in 1985. The two Catholic high schools at the old Columbus School building closed in 1990. The building, including the adjacent 1912 library branch building, was converted and reopened as Columbus Court market-rate housing in 1997. Even the Michelangelo School closed in 1989, leaving only one public school, the Eliot, in the North End. Although it took more than a decade, the Michelangelo School was converted into housing for seniors and was reopened as Villa Michelangelo in 2001.

Community leaders were able to bring about positive opportunities for North End senior citizens in the 1970s. The younger generation, however, had to grapple with different issues during that turbulent decade. Recreational drug usage rose among young people in the late 1960s and into the 1970s, as did a general mistrust of established authorities. Vagrancy, vandalism, graffiti and late-night noise all increased in the North End. Fewer youths participated in the religious processions associated with the summer feasts. Scattered artists and yuppies began to move into the neighborhood, and the first condominium conversions appeared in the early 1970s. With most of the fishing boats gone and many of the factories closing down, the North End's waterfront was losing its vitality. By the time of the Bicentennial, it was clear that the neighborhood was no longer inhabited solely by Italian Americans. Furthermore, the North End, like the rest of the city, would have to embrace change to ensure its future prosperity.

THE NORTH END TODAY

In July 2006, the cafés along Hanover Street left their doors and windows open so the crowds of soccer fans could watch the World Cup on their flat-screen televisions. Italy was playing France in the final game for the championship, and the spectators grew so numerous on both sides of Hanover Street that the people on one side literally backed into the posteriors of the people flowing from the other side. The police had to close Hanover Street to vehicular traffic, and when Italy prevailed, thousands of people shouted from the streets, the cafés and the apartment windows. The people gathered in the North End for the World Cup were not all locals or Italians, nor were they mostly dedicated soccer fans. But they all knew that the proper place to be in the Boston area to publicly show your support of, and pride in, Italy was the North End. Even after some thirty years of gentrification, the North End is still "Little Italy" in the popular imagination. Not everyone who lives there, however, can claim Italian heritage.

About one-third of the approximately ten thousand people who currently live in the North End are Italian or descended from Italians. Though there are far fewer Italian Americans in the North End as compared to a generation ago, those who still live in the neighborhood generally consider themselves the only true "North Enders," and few people would disagree. The Italian Americans who were born and raised in the North End, who attended the local schools and churches, who rehabilitated the buildings and politically protected the area, deserve to be known as authentic North Enders. If not for their efforts, the neighborhood might have long ago completely succumbed to redevelopment. In addition, all of the activities, programs and politics of the North End are still dominated by Italian Americans. The Little League, chamber of commerce, youth programs and the neighborhood council are led by Italian Americans (although some of these individuals are not originally from the North End), and the same heritage is shared by the district's city councilor, state representative and state senator.

There has been tension between North Enders and newcomers, going back to the late 1960s and 1970s. Back then, Fred Langone and his supporters advocated for senior housing as a way to redevelop the Commercial Street and Atlantic Avenue areas. However, real estate investors wanted to build luxury condominiums for the growing number of people interested in moving to the waterfront, which was being redeveloped with the New England Aquarium, Harbor Towers and other construction along Boston Harbor. For a long time, a split existed between the North End and the Waterfront. Residents of both areas were able to overcome much of the acrimony, however, and today many local community groups begin their names with "North End/ Waterfront." Everyone had to come together in the late 1980s and early 1990s to help protect the quality of life in the neighborhood because of the highway reconstruction project adjacent to the North End.

Rose Kennedy Greenway, looking northwest toward the new Zakim Bridge.

Standing in the beautiful Rose Kennedy Greenway parks that straddle Hanover Street, below Cross, it is already difficult to recall the feeling of walking beneath the old elevated expressway, even though it has only been gone a few years. The elevated highway was always noisy and stinking of exhaust, and it had a dingy pedestrian tunnel underneath it, which had to be traversed by people wishing to get to the North End from the Haymarket area. The federally funded construction project to remove the highway, known as the "Big Dig," included two new underground traffic tunnels, a harbor tunnel and a bridge. The final cost was approximately $15 billion, more than three times the original budget. The process of building a new underground highway and subsequently dismantling the elevated road was itself disruptive and unhealthy. Traffic was rerouted, pedestrian access was limited, North End businesses were hard to get to and therefore lost customers—and some had to completely close. It was not uncommon to be told that you had to walk home underneath a different section of the highway, usually dripping dirty water on your head, than the one you had used to go to work in the morning.

Rose Fitzgerald Kennedy (1890–1995) of Garden Court Street, 1916. She is shown here with her firstborn child, Joseph. Rose's second child, John Fitzgerald Kennedy, was the youngest person and the first Catholic to be elected president of the United States, in 1960. *Courtesy of the Boston Public Library, Print Department.*

The old highway was insulated with asbestos and coated with lead paint, so even though precautions were taken to wrap each section before it was cut and carted away, many wondered what might be floating in the air and into their lungs. Local residents attended countless meetings to help influence the project in small ways. For example, they helped to set times when noise could begin and should end; insisted on special windows to protect abutting buildings from excessive dust and noise; and alerted state and construction officials to local schedules for feasts, special events, and other times when Big Dig workers would need to be sensitive to community activities. The opportunity to give input was not afforded to North Enders when buildings were destroyed and the highway was originally built beginning in the late 1940s. Although the process looked much different four decades later, North Enders still had to endure nearly twenty years of the Big Dig. At least the project brought people from different parts of the neighborhood together, and everyone hopes that they will now have time to enjoy the new parkland without the intrusion of new mega-projects.

Real estate development is still a major issue confronting the neighborhood today. Investors don't spend millions of dollars to renovate a building, or build

Rose Kennedy Greenway, looking southeast.

a new structure, only to rent or sell the units below market-rate. Therefore, most of the recycled buildings or new construction on the waterfront is high-end retail and luxury housing. Even in the oldest parts of the North End, $350 or $400 per square foot for housing is still considered a good deal. In the luxury housing on Atlantic Avenue, or new construction on Fleet, Prince or Commercial Streets, the cost is often three or four times as much as the older condominiums. The situation is likely to continue, however, as long as there are local property owners who want to profit from the land and buildings they have inherited, as well as newcomers willing to pay the high prices. The inevitable result is that the Italian culture of the North End will continue to disappear, just like the Irish culture of the 1800s and the English culture before that. The working-class nature of the neighborhood is also all but gone. There are no shops left on Charter Street and very few remaining on Prince or Endicott. Most of the smaller streets in the area no longer have commercial activity either. The newer residents can afford to buy food, clothing, housewares and anything else from wherever they please, especially online. The North End no longer needs the many bakeries, candy shops, clothing stores or butchers it once had.

Tourism is one business that has thrived over the last thirty years. On April 18, 2008, Paul Revere's House celebrated its first one hundred years as a museum. The Paul Revere Memorial Association, the entity that owns the historic house and educates hundreds of thousands of people each year, plans to expand its facilities in the near future. The staff does an excellent job fostering new research on Paul Revere and his role in history. The Old North Church is the most frequented site on the entire Freedom Trail, and the image of its steeple graces the cover of the best Boston guidebooks. Old North is also a functioning Episcopal church, with regular services every Sunday and special observances for holidays and other occasions throughout the year. Tourists and out-of-towners also support more than one hundred Italian restaurants and a handful of boutiques in the compact neighborhood, with the vast majority along or near Hanover Street. People line up early on the sidewalks in front of the most popular bakeries and eateries year-round and taxicabs choke the street every weekend night.

The hundreds of thousands of visitors, the older North Enders, young professionals, college students, empty-nesters, business owners and families with young children all keep the neighborhood lively, interesting and one of the safest districts in the entire city. Locals still grapple with the issues of real estate development, dog waste and litter on the streets, noise from parties and businesses, liquor licenses and limited parking. But clean streets, the rights of business owners versus residents, quarrels over the best use of the land

Left: The Old North Church Gift Shop on Salem Street was built as the Protestant Chapel of St. Francis of Assisi in 1918 to serve a group of Italian Protestants in a neighborhood that was at the time otherwise Catholic or Jewish. Two lions guard the original entrance, and there is still a cross at the top of the building, though it is obscured in this image. The Old North Church is at the left.

Below: Paul Revere's House, built circa 1680, as seen from inside its courtyard. This is the oldest building in the North End, and it is the only surviving example of seventeenth-century architecture in downtown Boston. It is open for tours daily.

Copp's Hill Burying Ground, facing Hull Street. The famous steeple of the Old North Church is seen rising above the rear portion of the Villa Michelangelo housing complex. This is Boston's second-oldest cemetery, and it is the final resting place of William Copp, Increase Mather, Prince Hall, Thomas Lewis and thousands of others.

The sanctuary of the Old North Church, Boston's oldest church building, holds Episcopalian services every Sunday, and it is open for visitors daily.

and culture clashes are nothing new to the North End. The neighborhood is in a transitional period, and its future identity is still uncertain. Will it become a completely residential area with the exception of a strip of Italian restaurants? Will North Enders move to make the neighborhood a legally preserved historic district like Beacon Hill or Back Bay? Will a future group of immigrants carve out a space for itself in some corner of the community? What is certain is that any new iteration of the North End will exist in the same space as those of the past. For now, Italian Americans still lead the neighborhood, older North Enders watch over everyone from the street corners and apartment windows and all residents hear ancient church bells ring on Sundays and see the daily waves of tourists looking for Paul Revere and good *cannoli*. The North End is, and hopefully will continue to be, an authentic, historical and unique urban community.

SELECTED BIBLIOGRAPHY

Acts and Resolves of the Province of the Massachusetts Bay, 1692–1780. Boston: Wright & Potter, 1869–1886.

Bacon, Edwin M. *Bacon's Dictionary of Boston*. Cambridge, MA: Riverside Press, 1886.

Bailyn, Bernard. *The Ordeal of Thomas Hutchinson*. Cambridge, MA: Belknap Press of Harvard University Press, 1974.

Bell, J.L., and the Bostonian Society. "5th of November in Boston." Available online at http://display.5thofnovember.us/ (accessed March 16, 2008).

Boston Board of Aldermen. Minutes and Petitions. Boston City Archives.

Boston City Planning Board. *The North End: A Survey and a Comprehensive Plan*. Boston: City of Boston Printing Department, 1919.

Boston Common Council. Records. Boston City Archives.

Boston Port and Seamen's Aid Society. *Life of Father Taylor: The Sailor Preacher*. Boston: Boston Port and Seamen's Aid Society, 1904.

Boston 200 and Boston's Fourth of July Inc. *Boston Celebrates July '76*. Danbury, NH: Addison House, 1976.

Christ Church in the City of Boston. "The Fall and Rise of the Steeple, 1954–1955." Unpublished scrapbook.

Colesworthy, D.C. *John Tileston's School*. Boston: Antiquarian Book Store, 1887.

Colonial Society of Massachusetts. *Publications of the Colonial Society of Massachusetts*. Vol. 1. Boston: Colonial Society of Massachusetts, 1895.

DeMarco, William M. *Ethnics and Enclaves: Boston's Italian North End*. Ann Arbor: University of Michigan Research Press, 1981.

Durant, Henry F. *Defence of the Use of the Bible in Public Schools. Argument of Henry F. Durant, Esq., in the Eliot School Case*. Boston: Ticknor and Fields, 1859.

Ehrenfried, Albert. *A Chronicle of Boston Jewry: From the Colonial Settlement to 1900*. (Boston?): Irving Bernstein, 1963.

Eliot, John. *A Biographical Dictionary*. Boston: Edward Oliver, 1809.

Fischer, David Hackett. *Paul Revere's Ride*. New York: Oxford University Press, 1994.

Forbes, Esther. *Paul Revere And the World He Lived In*. Boston: Houghton Mifflin Company, 1942.

Goldfeld, Alex. "The History of the Streets of Boston's North End." Master's thesis, University of Massachusetts, 2007.

Goss, Elbridge Henry. *The Life of Colonel Paul Revere*. Boston: J.G. Cupples, 1891.

Hall, Michael G. *The Last American Puritan: The Life of Increase Mather, 1639–1723*. Middletown, CT: Wesleyan University Press, 1988.

Handlin, Oscar. *Boston's Immigrants, 1790–1880: A Study in Acculturation*. Revised and enlarged edition. Cambridge, MA: Belknap Press of Harvard University Press, 1991.

Herring, Joseph. "Arthur Buckminster Fuller." In *Dictionary of Unitarian and Universalist Biography*. Available online at http://www25temp.uua.org/uuhs/duub/articles/arthurbuckminsterfuller.html (accessed January 26, 2007).

Higginbotham, A. Leon, Jr. *In the Matter of Color: Race and the American Legal Process: The Colonial Period*. New York: Oxford University Press, 1980.

Jacobs, Jane. *The Death and Life of Great American Cities*. Revised edition. New York: Modern Library, 1993.

Langone, Fred. *The North End: Where It All Began*. Boston: Post-Gazette, 1994.

Lankevich, George J. *Boston: A Chronological and Documentary History, 1602–1970*. Dobbs Ferry, NY: Oceana Publications, 1974.

Lord, Robert H., John E. Sexton and Edward T. Harrington. *History of the Archdiocese of Boston, 1604–1943. In Three Volumes*. Cambridge, MA: Riverside Press, 1944.

Massachusetts Court of Assistants. *Records of the Court of Assistants of the Colony of the Massachusetts Bay*. Boston: County of Suffolk, 1904.

Mather, Cotton. *Diary of Cotton Mather*. New York: Frederick Ungar Publishing Company, 1911.

———. *Magnalia Christi Americana*. Hartford, CT: Silas Andrus and Son, 1855.

———. *Memorable Providences, Relating to Witchcrafts and Possessions*. Boston: Richard Pierce, 1689.

———. *The Negro Christianized*. Boston: Bartholomew Green, 1706.

McGreevy, John T. *Catholicism and American Freedom: A History*. New York: W.W. Norton & Company, 2003.

Morgan, Edmund S. *The Stamp Act Crisis: Prologue to Revolution*. Chapel Hill: University of North Carolina Press, 1995.

Paul Revere Memorial Association. *Paul Revere: Artisan, Businessman, and Patriot: The Man Behind the Myth*. Boston: Paul Revere Memorial Association, 1988.

Porter, Joseph W., ed. *The Bangor Historical Magazine*. Vol. 7. Bangor: Charles H. Glass & Company, 1892.

Quincy, Josiah. *The Journals of Major Samuel Shaw, The First American Consul at Canton*. Boston: William Crosby and H.P. Nichols, 1847.

Robbins, Chandler. *A History of the Second Church, or Old North, in Boston. To Which is Added, A History of the New Brick Church*. Boston: John Wilson & Son, 1852.

Schneider, Eric C. *In the Web of Class: Delinquents and Reformers in Boston, 1810s–1930s*. New York: New York University Press, 1992.

Sewall, Samuel. *The Selling of Joseph: A Memorial*. Boston: Bartholomew Green and John Allen, 1700.

Stebbins, Emma. *Charlotte Cushman: Her Letters and Memories of Her Life*. Cambridge, MA: Riverside Press, 1878.

Suffolk County Deeds. Books 1–14. Boston: City of Boston, 1880–1906.

Suffolk County Deeds. Suffolk County (Massachusetts) Registry of Deeds.

Thomas, M. Halsey, ed. *The Diary of Samuel Sewall*. New York: Farrar, Straus and Giroux, 1973.

Tudor, William, ed. *Deacon Tudor's Diary*. Boston: Wallace Spooner, 1896.

Whitehill, Walter Muir. *Boston Public Library: A Centennial History*. Cambridge, MA: Harvard University Press, 1956.

Whitmore, William H., ed. *Report(s) of the Record Commissioners of the City of Boston*. Boston: Rockwell and Churchill, 1876–1896.

Zobel, Hiller B. *The Boston Massacre*. New York: W.W. Norton & Company, 1996.

Index

ABOUT THE AUTHOR

For nearly a decade, Alex R. Goldfeld has been creating and leading tours of Boston's historic neighborhoods, most notably the North End, Beacon Hill and Roxbury. He has conducted research and assisted in planning for local organizations, including the Nichols House Museum, the First Church in Roxbury and the Vilna Shul. Goldfeld also served as director of operations at Boston's Museum of African American History, where he oversaw the visitor experience, managed the historic sites and facilitated tours of the Black Heritage Trail. He holds a Master of Arts in History from the University of Massachusetts Boston and lives with his family in the North End.

Please visit us at
www.historypress.net